New Visions and
New Voices

New Visions and New Voices

Extending the Principles of Archetypal Pedagogy to Include a Variety of Venues, Issues, and Projects

Volume 2

Edited by

Clifford Mayes
Jacquelyn Ane Rinaldi

ROWMAN & LITTLEFIELD
Lanham • Boulder • New York • London

Published by Rowman & Littlefield
An imprint of The Rowman & Littlefield Publishing Group, Inc.
4501 Forbes Boulevard, Suite 200, Lanham, Maryland 20706
www.rowman.com

86-90 Paul Street, London EC2A 4NE, United Kingdom

British Library Cataloguing in Publication Information Available

Library of Congress Cataloging-in-Publication Data

Names: Mayes, Clifford, editor. | Rinaldi, Jacquelyn Ane, editor.
Title: New visions and new voices : extending the principles of archetypal pedagogy
   to include a variety of venues, issues, and projects / edited by Clifford Mayes and
   Jacquelyn Ane Rinaldi.
Description: Lanham : Rowman & Littlefield, [2021] | Includes bibliographical
   references and index. | Summary: "This book takes the principles of archetypal
   pedagogy and applies them in exciting new ways to fields as diverse as literary
   studies, therapy and, of course, teacher education"—Provided by publisher.
Identifiers: ISBN 9781475870084 (v. 2 ; cloth) | ISBN 9781475870091
   (v. 2 ; paper) | ISBN 9781475870107 (ePub)
Subjects: LCSH: Educational psychology. | Archetype (Psychology) | Critical pedagogy.
Classification: LCC LB1051 .N428 2021 (print) | LCC LB1051 (ebook) | DDC
   370.15—dc23
LC record available at https://lccn.loc.gov/2021032093
LC ebook record available at https://lccn.loc.gov/2021032094

Contents

Introduction

This volume, the second in a series titled *New Visions and New Voices: Extending the Principles of Archetypal Pedagogy to Include a Variety of Venues, Issues, and Projects*, is a collection of essays by some of the most promising new scholars to emerge on the Jungian scene (in addition to my modest contributions). There are two reasons that these volumes are so exciting.

The first is that they contain some of the most recent work by some of the most cutting-edge new scholars in analytical psychology—Jung's term for what we now generally call Jungian psychology. That is already a significant enough event.

However, the second reason these two books may prove memorable is that they each revolve around archetypal pedagogy, which is not the primary research focus of these scholars, except for Kell, Schumacher, and Savage. But far from being a problem, this is all to the good, for it takes the principles and practices of archetypal pedagogy and applies them to a wide variety of fields. The cause of archetypal pedagogy is thus considerably strengthened, its stride fortuitously lengthened, and its audience augmented by this happy convergence of highly diverse chapters.

Ben Edwards, whose first major showing of his artwork moved the *New York Times* to call him "an instant classic," discusses with singular eloquence the problem that Jung confronted all his professional life—namely, how to re-symbolize a culture that has been de-symbolized, indeed de-sacralized, by the consequences of modernity and the quandaries of postmodernity. In a different vein, another visual artist, Alexa Gallo, the owner of a highly successful photography studio and also the founder of an approach to photography that she calls "archetypal photography," marshals the principles of archetypal pedagogy to approach dog training in a manner that is not only the most humane and respectful for the animals but psychospiritually salutary for their human partners.

Claire Savage and Cynthia Schumacher—both educators of sweeping vision in and for the classroom—invite us to imagine along with them some of the contours and colors of what an archetypal pedagogy looks like in action. Both of them, deeply steeped in the most recent Jungian and pedagogical theory while at the same time being veterans of the everyday classroom, perfectly answer to Dewey's ideal of the "scholar practitioner," in whom theory and practice are constantly informing and refining each other. As their focus is archetypal pedagogy, they are bound to advance the field in a special way as its new leaders, along with Kevin Kell.

Susan Persing and Vanessa Jankowski both engage in this book in what Jungian theory does with such special acuity—the analysis of myth. Indeed, it may be plausibly claimed that Jungian psychology began as the mythopoetic parsing of dreams, events, and emotions in a person's life. Dr. Jung, the psychiatrist but also scholar of ancient texts and languages, brought to the consulting room not only medical but also historical, literary, and philosophical skills and training to help heal the patient and send him or her out of the hell of neurosis and psychosis into a psychospiritually enriched world.

As did Jung himself, Persing and Jankowski aim at fostering a life of a dynamic stoicism and liberated creativity in the individual in every aspect of his or her life. Persing shows us how myth can have this curative effect by drawing on both her capacious knowledge of Jung's work and the exquisite literary flair in her writing. Jankowski, as adept at theory as she is in practice as the head of a psychotherapeutic clinic in Chicago, accomplishes the same goal with grace and conviction.

Kevin Kell and Jacquelyn Rinaldi are both superb clinicians who bring their professional insights to bear upon some of the most interesting but also most difficult issues in education. Most especially, they meet head on the primary problem of modern education. This dilemma is the co-opting of the schools by corporate interests into what the greatest of all U.S. education historians, Lawrence Cremin, called in 1988 the anti-democratic military-industrial-*educational* complex. In this indictment and warning and following President Eisenhower in his farewell address from the White House in 1961, when he spoke of the existence of a military-industrial complex, Cremin decried the grave threat to democracy posed by this anti-democratic pedagogy of conformity.

Rinaldi and Kell share President Eisenhower's concern and see the danger of the corporate mentality now creeping into the classroom in full serpentine form. This thereby changes the school from being a site for the cultivation of each student's unique individuation process (Rinaldi's psychological focus) and the cultivation of the immanent "pedagogical moment" (Kell's ontological concern). What the military-industrial-educational complex does is to turn the schools into a training ground for compliant droids in the new world order of global capitalism. Rinaldi, now completing the dissertation for her second doctorate in psychology, and Kell, a man whose talents as an artisan and opera singer deepen his calling as a psychotherapist by revealing new dimensions of experience to his clients, strive in both their writing and practice to foster the creativity in each patient—which was ever Jung's therapeutic and existential goal.

This volume concludes with my observations on one of the finest young American poets of the "Gen X" cohort, Kyle Jankowski. As I noted at the outset of my critical appreciation of his work "The Poet as a Teacher (in Unteachable Times)," Jankowski is thoroughly *sui generis*—a class of his own. He has the audacity (which is justified in his work only because of the enormity of his talent) to confront a daunting range of themes and topics and to marshal an impressive array of conventional literary styles as well as radically idiosyncratic ones. The result is that it is simply impossible to pin him down.

All that one can finally say about Jankowski is that Jankowski is Jankowski. For a lesser poet this would point to an aesthetics of narcissism—a sort of warmed over "confessional poetry" of the 1950s and 1960s. In Jankowski, however, it is evidence of his profound psychospiritual investment in everything he writes about—whether it is the poignant role of Poland, the country of his ancestors, in the West's greatest achievements or most abysmal failures, the loss of a salutary sense of chivalry in the general vulgarity and mess of postmodernism, or the persistent hope of communion with the archetypal realm in this de-sacralized epoch of history. And most compelling of all is how this emanates from his truly counter-cultural commitment to Roman Catholicism and the love of Our Lady, whose spirit infuses his work, but never in a self-absorbed or polemical but always in a generous and relevant way.

My colleagues and I hope that each reader will find in this volume things of psychospiritual worth in his or her own trek to the Divine in the archetypal forests of his or her own mind, psyche, and spirit.

Clifford Mayes
Las Vegas, Nevada
November 9, 2022

Chapter 1

A Crisis of Spirit

Archetypal Pedagogy and Cultural Revelation

Benjamin Edwards

THE SPIRIT OF PROPHECY AND THE PEDAGOGIC ACT

One day nearly three decades ago I wandered into an art museum and had the earthshaking fortune to witness the end of the world. I had never seen anything like it. The paintings were staged in nineteenth-century melodramatic fashion: set within stately wooden columns and voluptuous red velvet curtains were pictures of the five life-stages of a fictional civilization, from its wild dawn to its pitiful, whimpering twilight. My heroic, twenty-something ego, newly aware of the impending climate crisis, came face to face not just with my own mortality, or even my nation's, but the "running ahead into death" (Heidegger, 2008, p. 306) of an entire global civilization. Thomas Cole's *The Course of Empire* (1836) continues to haunt me to this day, as it must haunt all Americans, especially after January 6, 2021, when the world witnessed the first glimpse of truth in Cole's prophecy.

C. G. Jung (1969c), writing roughly one hundred years after Cole's masterpiece, put this confrontation with the dark side into words: "As a totality, the self is by definition always a *complexio oppositorum*, and the more consciousness insists on its own luminous nature and lays claim to moral authority, the more the self will appear as something dark and menacing" (p. 443). As Americans we want to cling to "greatness," even if it means snuggling up with our precious as we tumble mindlessly into the abyss. The Self, which for Jung (1968b) was the archetype of psychic wholeness and ultimately

1

indistinguishable from the God-image (p. 31), does not necessarily share the ego's idea of the good.

One of Jung's most controversial contributions to modern thought was to restore a mythological reckoning with the "dark" side of God. To deny the reality of this archetype, to adopt the Church's position of *privatio boni*—that evil is simply the absence of good—is to simply drive "evil" underground, into the unconscious, where it may fester and grow unnoticed until one day it is fatefully projected as shadow. One of the tragedies of the Western tradition is the idea that evil resides in the human choice to turn away from God and toward Satan. Those who do not conform to the orthodox view of the (patriarchal) God, that is, the heretics or "deviants," have historically borne the brunt of this unconscious projection. According to this toxic mentality, the problem is always *them*, never *us*. But there is an even deeper, more insidious problem, and that is *only* seeing the world as made up of an *us*, who must be right, and a *them*, who are always wrong. In short, a morally pure God-image automatically creates the need for an impure human scapegoat.

Americans have become all too familiar with this phenomenon of political and ideological polarization because its archetypal energy has passed the threshold of collective consciousness. As I've watched the world glide past Cole's middle stage, *The Consummation of Empire*, the gravity of stage four, *Destruction*, feels inexorable. The prospect of collapse has always seemed remote and external. After January 6, 2021, however, a clearer picture of societal tension has come into view. The problem is not purely ecological nor even economic; both are the material catalysts of a spiritual phenomenon. The problem is essentially psychological. A volatile clash of moral values and shadow projection, a *complexio oppositorum* (unity of opposites) amplified by the information age, threatens to burst our global machine at its seams.

Cole's depiction of the rise and fall of civilization was what we might call a pedagogic act. His vision carries archetypal resonance because his educational warning is still not only valid today but even more obviously urgent. Cole followed a long line of prophets who warned of their culture's perilous drift out of Tao, from the Old Testament prophets such as Isaiah, Jeremiah, and Ezekiel, to the kinder, gentler Jesus of the New Testament, and even to Romantic artists such as William Blake. Jung (1970b), especially late in life, positioned himself as such a prophet, going so far as to proclaim his "duty" to "prepare those few who will hear me for coming events which are in accord with the end of an era" (p. 311). Well versed in ancient tradition, and deeply conscious of the important psychic effects of transitioning from one "world age" to another, Jung believed that such moments herald important changes "in the constellation of psychic dominants, of the archetypes, or 'gods' as they used to be called, which bring about, or accompany, long-lasting transformations of the collective psyche" (p. 311).

WHOLENESS AND ARCHETYPAL PEDAGOGY

The ego's confrontation with the Self, the archetype of wholeness, is far from peaches and cream. *Wholeness* is one of those words that sounds nice—who doesn't like wholeness in the abstract?—but when real, live shadow comes knocking, the harbinger of wholeness is equally the prophet of doom, because the stability the ego so desperately craves is no longer suited to new cultural and technological paradigms. Those who bear pedagogic acts also expose inconvenient truths, and for those individuals and societies too morally pure to listen, or too quick to deny their own shadow, these heralds of change are simply too uncomfortable to bear.

Prophetic figures like Cole and Jung provide the traditional models for a burgeoning field in education called archetypal pedagogy, founded by Jungian scholar Clifford Mayes. Mayes (2017) promotes "teaching and learn-ing for wholeness," insisting that working with archetypes in self-narratives is a "salvific" and redemptive endeavor. Not only that, incorporating a Jungian approach to education is vital to restoring its sacred mission, which is to foster critical, free thinking and questioning citizens in the service of a healthy, functioning democracy. Mayes (2020) is forthright about archetypal pedagogy as a form of "cultural resistance" (p. 178) in the face of an increas-ingly technocratic and hyper-efficient factory approach: "Jungian pedagogy can serve as a powerful tool in resisting the hegemonic corporate approach to education, which determines a good deal of schooling today" (2017, p. 14). Mayes (2020) sees archetypal pedagogy as a restoration and renewal of what John Dewey once envisioned, where classrooms are "the principal sites where the sacred world-historical mission of democracy was advanced" (p. 48). To put it bluntly, if we don't save education, then we can't save democracy.

While traditional education takes place in the classroom, it can never be an activity that stops with a diploma. Every individual in a democracy has a sacred duty to engage in a life of ongoing self-education beyond the class-room. In a world that increasingly values efficiency, technological "disrup-tion," and maximizing profit over personal welfare and safety, it is all too easy to sacrifice the hard work that self-education entails. When the collective no longer seems to value such work, when the culture falls into what Mircea Eliade (1957) called "profane time," then it becomes even more difficult for individuals to buck societal pressures and take this mission upon themselves. American culture itself, not just its citizens, needs redemption.

In this essay, I follow the prescription for spiritual renewal forged by Mayes in *Archetypes, Culture, and the Individual in Education: Three Pedagogical Narratives* (2020), laying out a two-step process for cultural redemption. In medical terms, the first step is meant to stop the bleeding, to diagnose and excise the cancer that has so polarized American culture. This process is what I call *easing the binary* of ego and shadow. The ego tends to see things in black and white terms, especially morality. The unconscious, however, doesn't operate in binary terms; in fact, it actively seeks to undermine such a narrow worldview. In Jungian terms, the unconscious is *compensatory* to the one-sided attitude of the ego.

The first step in de-escalating the egoic conflicts ravaging the culture today is prerequisite to the second step: *rejuvenating the symbol*. The symbol is a mysterious psychic object that magnetically attracts energy and hope because it is pregnant with meaning (Jung, 1971, p. 475), even if it is not totally understandable or even ever knowable on a conscious level. That is not a weakness, but the source of its great strength. The "numinous" symbol (*numen* is Latin for spirit or divine power) guides us to a wholeness that is so desperately needed for psychic health, whether for an individual, a community, a nation, even a global village. The master key to both steps one and two is personal revelation, which is the archetype of growth, change, and the expansion of consciousness. Individuals must learn to seek this not for themselves, but for the very survival of their community and a strong, resilient, and cohesive social fabric.

I. EASING THE BINARY

Is Cultural Compensation Still Possible?

In Jungian psychology, the Self spontaneously manifests through images of wholeness as a compensatory principle to a dangerously one-sided ego to restore psychic balance. The ego, however, along with its cultural extensions, tends to remain blind to the flashing alarms until it's too late. Individuals generally do not seek therapy until a problem has developed into a crisis. When things are going well, the ego is perfectly fine thinking that it's running the show. The minute things take a turn for the worse, however, the God-image appears, along with helpless pleas for explanations. Why is this happening to me? What can I do about it? How can I get back on track with my life? Since therapy often involves uncomfortable work on oneself, and openness to change, the ego naturally resists. The crisis becomes apparent: the soul wants change while the ego requires stability, and the individual is caught in the middle. The desire for the new is exciting but also terrifying because change always involves risk. The process of therapy is learning to engage in a meaningful dialog with these opposites. The individual's perspective changes. The question is no longer one of returning to an old way of doing things and dwelling on the past. The new way forward may be dark and mysterious because it is unknown, but it also offers opportunities to change one's narrative and create a meaningful self.

Therapy, or a dialog of self facilitated by a trained therapist, is the individual's way of de-escalating a psychic split. Nations have no therapists, though Jung (1966) believed artists try to adopt this role. The artist's "lack of adaptation" to collective values

> enables him to follow his own yearnings far from the beaten path, and to discover what it is that would meet the unconscious needs of his age. Thus, just as the one-sidedness of the individual's conscious attitude is corrected by reactions from the unconscious, so art represents a process of self-regulation in the life of nations and epochs. (p. 83)

Cole's pedagogical act is a Jungian compensatory act directed at a dangerously one-sided collective identity.

History has shown, however, that the nation, and now global industrial culture, has continually ignored the compensatory messages from the unconscious. When this happens to an individual, writes Jung (1968b),

> the presumption of the ego can only be damped down by moral defeat. This is necessary, because otherwise one will never attain that median degree of modesty which is essential for the maintenance of a balanced state. It is not a question, as one might think, of relaxing morality itself but of *making a moral effort in a different direction.* (p. 25, emphasis mine)

If the arts and humanities are no longer sufficient to compensate the one-sided values of a STEM-drunk culture, and the one-sided inflation continues to escalate to dangerous levels, then how is compensation to occur without catastrophe? Is it even possible? Are the arts and humanities in themselves capable of such cultural compensation? Have they ever truly performed this function, or have they rather witnessed and expressed the conscience of the age, offering possible alternative worlds while doing little or nothing to actively change the society from which they spring? The sculptor Carl Andre proposed an archetypal model for the artist when he said, "Culture is something that is done to us. Art is something we do to culture" (cited in Hyde, 2010, p. 307). This is a noble, empowering sentiment, a rallying cry for revolutionary artists everywhere, but is it truly effective, or *affective*? That is, does art actively change the culture, or do its alternative worlds, like dreams and their affects, make the possibility of change perceptible?

Individuals and movements who attempt to adopt the compensatory shadow-values of the Self will be necessarily viewed with suspicion, even hostility, by the dominant ego-values of the culture. This is complicated by the fact that American culture itself is dangerously polarized along mostly urban and rural but also educational divides. There is not one set of dominant ego-values, but two, and they are diametrically opposed. In the media this is commonly referred to as the "culture wars," and these battles are escalating. The shadow-values of the Self are split because the culture is split; one cannot adopt a compensatory position without taking a side in the battle between ego and soul, which threatens to make "wholeness" a chimerical fantasy. How, then, do individuals, who Jung (1970a, p. 271) believed are the sole carriers of consciousness, go about balancing a symmetrically hyper-charged bipolar culture without appearing "dark and menacing," or worse, as advocating for "moral defeat"? In other words, how do we avoid the violence of dialectic in favor of the de-escalation of dialog? What is the process by which individuals may work together constructively to make "a moral effort in a different direction"? And what are these different moral directions?

Values and the Cultural Unconscious

As the archetypal psychologist James Hillman (1975) has observed, "We are always in the embrace of an idea," which is also to say that we always adopt a mythic and archetypal stance in relation to our culture and its values (p. 121). The problem with this, as Kenneth Burke so eloquently put it, is that "a way of seeing is also a way of not seeing" (cited in Coupe, 2005, pp. 25, 69). Philosophically, these ideas are not new. Martin Heidegger (1971) long ago saw that truth-as-disclosure—what he called *aletheia* (bringing out of oblivion), as opposed to truth-as-correspondence—is simultaneously revealing *and* concealing: "Truth, in its nature, is un-truth" (pp. 53–54). Neuroscience has since shown that a way of seeing tends to become entrenched. The thalamus, positioned between the eyes and the visual cortex, provides us with an internal model of the world. When we perceive what's "out there" the visual cortex gets information from the eyes, but it gets *ten times more information from the thalamus* (Eagleman, 2015, pp. 56–57). This means that we are literally projecting our view of the world onto what we see: our internal model—especially our language, the underlying structural grammar of consciousness—defines and limits our ability to perceive. The more we cling to our truths, the more we become blinded by them.

Like complexes, we do not have these ideological positions—these mythic stances—as much as they have us. Jung (1968b) believed that the feeling-toned complexes that erupt from the unconscious and grip the ego are inherently personal, residing in the personal unconscious, while their essential core or underlying energy is of a transpersonal, archetypal nature, coming from the collective unconscious (p. 4). Jungian analyst Joseph Henderson (1990) proposed a middle layer between these two, what he called the cultural unconscious (p. 117). If *complexes* are personal, and *archetypes* transpersonal (and transcultural), then *values* are inherently cultural because they relate the individual to the collective. Henderson writes that

> insofar as the personal shadow is the opposite, *not of the whole ego but only of the persona*, it always has a social (and therefore cultural) aspect, since the persona embodies our need for appropriate social interaction. Therefore, a study of unconscious cultural conditioning may become an absolute necessity in order to understand certain projections that people make upon each other. (p. 112, emphasis in original)

Values, which always tie together the personal and the archetypal, must operate at some scale of culture, from the local to the global. Here, however, we run into the twin problems of relativism and nihilism, a dilemma first presented to philosophy when Nietzsche proclaimed the death of God. If values are relative to culture, then they are also relative to hegemony and power. But values cannot be *purely* cultural because they mediate the personal, and therefore relative, subjective psyche and the collective objective psyche. Cultural values are, paradoxically, archetypally bipolar, which is to say that they have both relative and absolute moral aspects. The problem is, in modernity all values manifest first through the individual, at the relative end of the spectrum. This is a crisis of authority that global culture has not yet mastered. How are we to know if these personal convictions are morally right?

For Jung (1968a), the paradox is "one of our most valuable spiritual possessions, while uniformity of meaning is a sign of weakness" (pp. 15–16). The archetype of the Self, containing all the opposites, as well as their synthesis, at all levels of being, is the archetype of paradox *par excellence* (p. 19). Consequently, the archetype of the Self does not provide answers to the individual, but questions. The *opus contra naturam*, or work of spirit against the enigma of blind nature, is the individual's task. Bringing unconscious contents to the scrutiny of consciousness is a moral duty that Jung (1968c) called the process of individuation (p. 40). Through the study of archetypes at the core of personal complexes and cultural values, individuals gain insight into ways of seeing and behaving that might either go unnoticed or simply seem natural. For Heidegger (2008), this "natural" mode is following what *Das Man*, or the "they-self" does, because that is the way it has always been done (p. 307). The individual runs the risk of being inauthentic by not coming to terms with one's own mortality and unique selfhood. For both Jung and Heidegger, consciousness expands and grows only by turning away from the default position of collective values and coming to know and embracing one's own individuality as expressing something uniquely other. The promise of individuation and authenticity is nothing short of spiritual liberation. We know that consciousness develops at the level of the individual. But is individuation possible at the cultural level without violence, economic disruption, or ecological distress?

The events of January 6th, as well as the continuing escalations in the "culture wars" over such issues as critical race theory (CRT), do not inspire confidence that American culture can come to terms with its various shadows without violent conflict. Individuals may be the carriers of consciousness, but they are also the carriers of the cultural unconscious. Revolutionary technologies such as the Internet, the smart phone, social media, and extreme content-pushing algorithms have created a potent and seductive cocktail that taps into the god of fear known to neuroscience as the amygdala. This fear polarizes and exacerbates the blind, instinctual ego-shadow dynamic, further entrenching moral values and ossifying our respective internal models, making them resistant to change. One cannot even begin to think of having a dialog with the other when that other is the devil incarnate. This is the inevitable flip side to the righteousness and inflexibility of one's own luminous moral position. The crisis of the present age is a crisis of moral authority. While individuals carry consciousness of values, they cluster together into cultural camps, or tribes, and this collectivity reinforces their power as cultural complexes, thus intensifying their "psychic gravity" and nullifying individuation or authenticity. Long ago Jung identified this problem, as well as possible solutions, but for various reasons the modern world has largely ignored his insights, leading us to the crisis we face today.

Dialectics, Antinomies, and the Transcendent Function

Perhaps Jung's greatest contribution to both psychology and philosophy was his insight that the ego tends to become morally polarized, and that the unconscious seeks to compensate this one-sided attitude in the Self's quest for psychic wholeness. Technically, it is the persona, or the outer face of the ego that adopts the polarized position, which then relegates its opposite to the shadow. The ego's inner aspect, the soul, seeks to restore this broken-off aspect of the Self. This is why Jung's thought is so relevant to us today. His brilliance lay in his vast breadth of knowledge—mythic, ancient, esoteric, religious, philosophical, scientific—and his ability to synthesize disparate strands of psychic insight into a coherent vision that speaks to our modern and postmodern sensibilities. He achieved this insight during a period of personal crisis, when he attempted to forge his own psychological vision to contrast with Freud's. Many of his therapeutic approaches, however, have been eclipsed by two factors: first, the prominence of Freud's psychoanalysis, which reductively seeks to neutralize the neurotic effects of the shadow, thus fortifying the ego; and second, the absolute dominance of Marxist thought in the 20th century, which reduced Hegel's spiritual dialectic into a materialist operation of history. Both movements deviated from their ancient roots, shifting the emphasis from a process of open-ended growth to a goal-oriented endeavor. Jung's psychology in many ways restores the dialectic of thesis-antithesis-synthesis back to the Romantic conception of Schelling, which sought to reunify what Kant had torn asunder when he firmly separated the objective (phenomenal) and subjective (noumenal) worlds, whereby the former is empirical and knowable while the latter is transcendent and essentially unprovable. The key to Kant's separation was the concept of the antinomy, or conflict of equally compelling laws, which come from these two separate spheres.

The problem of moral antinomies is an ancient one, and with a little philosophical detective work one may trace them back through some of Jung's other influences. The Christian mystic Jacob Boehme, with his vision of the wrath and light of God mixed in the natural world (a concept derived from Kabbalah and the two pillars of God), was a profound influence on Schelling, Hegel, and later Jung. Nicolas of Cusa, with the idea that God provides the coincidence of opposites in nature, directly inspired Jung's vision of the Self as a *complexio oppositorum*. And the very concept of dialectics as means to philosophical wisdom goes back to Plato's Socratic dialogues. In one of the later dialogues, the *Statesman* (trans. 1952), Plato articulates the problem of moral antinomies when he observes that there is not one unified virtue, but parts of virtue that may come into conflict, such as courage and moderation (306bc). Not only that, when they appear together, they *must* come into conflict (307c). Such conflict, moreover, is human nature because "men react to situations in one way or another according to their dispositions. They favor some forms of action as being akin to their own character, and they recoil from acts arising from opposite tendencies as being foreign to themselves" (307d). The role of the statesman, according to Plato, is to be a "kingly weaver" and blend these opposites into the "web of state" (310e). This higher self must entrust the various offices of state to be shared by both (311a).

This notion of the mediating third between polar opposites was central to ancient thought, in both the West and the East (Taoist philosophy viewed humanity as mediating between Heaven and Earth). Hegel (inspired by Boehme) applied this ancient concept to the dialectic, giving it an upward thrust. Spirit, he said, wanted to manifest in nature so that it may realize its full potential. For the alchemists (along with Boehme) this process was called *inqualiren*; for Hegel it was *Aufheben*, which has such contradictory meanings as "lifting up," "abolish," "suspend," and "transcend." Jung (1969d) adopted the idea and adapted it to psychological language, calling it the "transcendent function," arising "from the union of conscious and unconscious contents" (p. 69). By engaging with dream or fantasy material in physical form, and by holding the tension of the opposites (specifically aesthetics versus meaning), a new, higher level of consciousness results that compensates each of the opposites of the antinomy, thus neutralizing the conflict by grow-ing out of it (p. 85). In translating this philosophical insight into psychologi-cal terms, Jung envisioned a fourfold structure of the Self, much inspired by Boehme. The ego offers a yes, while the shadow offers a no (or vice versa), which creates a polarity. One may either rise above the conflict into higher consciousness and growth, or else descend into ignorance, thereby threaten-ing a potentially catastrophic psychic splitting of the personality.

All this seemingly abstract and esoteric philosophical material offered very real and practical results for psychology. From these insights Jung (1971) went on to formulate his theory of psychological types, now mostly known in popular culture as the forerunner to the Myers-Briggs system. Jung proposed that the ego, in its need to adapt to the outer world, came to rely heavily on one of four cognitive functions in either their introverted or extraverted capacities (thinking, feeling, intuition, and sensation). A dominant function, however, necessarily entails an inferior, or shadow, function. Jung paired these as two sets of antinomies: one could either be a thinking or a feeling type, but not both; one could be an intuitive or a sensing type, but not both. Extreme one-sidedness in the dominant function will constellate and extreme reaction in the unconscious on the part of the shadow function. When the shadow remains unconscious, it is inevitably projected onto any convenient "hook" that crosses the ego's path. Psychological conflict is the inevitable result. One may then either remain stuck in ignorance or engage in the diffi-cult psychological work of growth and transformation, which is the revelation of new consciousness.

One of Jung's greatest errors was his assignment of gender roles to the functions of thinking (men were superior in their Logos capacity) and feel-ing (women were more attuned to Eros). Very few would subscribe to such views today. When Jung (1969b) proposes that *"perfection* is a masculine desideratum, while woman inclines by nature to *completeness"* (p. 395) we must, in my view, strip this statement of its gender stereotyping and instead look to the archetypal antinomy itself. Yahweh, says Jung, has lost sight of his unknown consort, Sophia. He is only motivated by *perfection* and has relegated *completeness* to the shadow. The Self, or the God-image, is itself a *complexio oppositorum* that ever exists in dynamic tension between these two conflicting moral imperatives. The task of consciousness is to negotiate this tension in a way that rises above nature's preferred method, which is boom and bust, and violent conflict. This division between "masculine" and "femi-nine" values is one that also appears in more recent psychological literature, also based on personality types.

The "Moral Matrix"

Social psychologist Jonathan Haidt (2012) offers an array of archetypal values that may be rooted in Jung's cognitive functions and ego attitudes. Haidt likens these values to moral taste buds. Building on the work of child psychologist Jean Piaget, Haidt proposes a series of moral foundations that gradually fall into place through development. Each positive value is paired with its negative: (1) Care/Harm, (2) Fairness/Cheating, (3) Loyalty/Betrayal, (4) Authority/Subversion, and (5) Sanctity/Degradation (pp. 151–179). Upon reflection and after discussion with colleagues, Haidt added a sixth foundation, Liberty/Oppression (pp. 197–205). This addition demonstrates that as culture changes, new prominent archetypes may emerge into collective consciousness. History shows that the emergence of new moral values may be accompanied by horrific violence and societal upheaval. For example, Liberty was not considered a moral value until the Enlightenment, and it took several revolutions before it was fully accepted. With the rise of technocratic authoritarianism and its need for order and national unity, however, Liberty is under threat. As compensation, global culture may now be witnessing the emergence of a new moral value: Diversity/Uniformity. This value runs directly counter to its antinomy, Unity/Fragmentation. Thus, our chief moral problem today is the ancient philosophical problem of the many and the one, or in modern terms, how to negotiate the dual needs of individual freedom and the communal good. *E pluribus unum* is under direct assault.

Haidt's research shows that political and religious affiliations have strong correspondences to certain values. Personality tests also show links between traits such as openness with some values but not others. Though his research does not include Jung's psychological types, it is not unreasonable to suppose that some of Jung's types are predisposed to particular values, making some dominant and others inferior. Haidt urges his readers to "step out of the moral Matrix" and try to understand different points of view when it comes to moral values. This implies that it is possible to become super-moral, or to transcend out of the conflicting opposites, or to use Jung's terminology, to achieve wholeness. And yet, for anyone who takes Haidt's online moral foundations quizzes, it quickly becomes apparent that it is not possible to do so.

It is not possible to achieve a "perfect score" on such a test, nor is it possible to fail. Rather, a person might appear one-sided, scoring very highly on some values, or conversely, they might seem relatively balanced, with an even distribution of values. When taking the quiz, clearly the most troublesome questions involve conflicting values, when one must choose between two that seem to have an equal claim. As Jung (1968b) observes, "the real moral problems spring from *conflicts of duty*" (p. 25, emphasis in original). In other words, these values are antinomies. The most obvious antinomy in

Haidt's spectrum is Authority/Subversion and Liberty/Oppression. What is legitimate authority for some is oppression for others, while at the same time revolutionary acts in the name of liberty are sometimes indistinguishable from subversion. Positive and negative poles of such values are relative to one's position in society, as well as to cultural norms.

What does this tell us about the psychological dilemma underlying Cole's paintings, as well as our own heated and sometimes violent debates in contemporary society? Boehme's mystical vision and Haidt's research show that it is humanly impossible to be "perfectly moral" because we are creatures of both ignorance and truth. As Jung observed about Yahweh, who was dynamically split between "perfection" (his value) and "completeness" (that of Sophia, his unknown consort), we too are split as a culture. It is no coincidence that Haidt's values fall along traditional party lines, with Democrats embodying the "feminine" values of Care, Fairness, and Liberty while Republicans strongly favor the stereotypically "masculine" Authority, Loyalty, and Sanctity.

An archetypal perspective shows that we are each limited in our own way, and we can only become conscious of those limitations by engaging in meaningful dialog with other types of people who represent values other than our own. That is what archetypal pedagogy, an engagement with inconvenient and uncomfortable wholeness, is all about. If modern technology, particularly social media, is a catalyst for conscious ego ossification, rigidity, and amplification—a dangerous trend given that the shadow and scapegoat projection grow simultaneously in the unconscious—then the logical extension of that trend is violent, dialectical confrontation. War has always been nature's preferred way of handling extreme human conflicts. The antidote for that is a dialog of humility and respect for alternate points of view, something an archetypal perspective can provide. Consciousness of the archetypes and their role in individual and cultural stories does not mean that we deny our own values, but it does force us to question them and to examine where we might be wrong. I do not believe it is desirable to hit all the values equally on Haidt's chart; doing so would mean a leveling down into some kind of waffling, moral mush. Nor do I believe one-sidedness is necessarily wrong; believing strongly in certain moral values over others means that an individual has convictions that are not easily broken. But clinging to values *unconsciously* without self-examination is the very definition of ignorance. Such ignorance is what leads to the dangerous binary of ego and shadow, righteousness and projection. The antidote to unconscious ignorance is conscious revelation, the knowledge that as individuals we are not whole and *can never be on our own*, not without the other. Revelation does not allow us to step out of the "moral Matrix," rather, it lifts our world up into a more perfect, and more *complete* union.

II. REJUVENATING THE SYMBOL

The Communal Object

The crisis of moral authority—the dual problems of extreme relativism and radical individualism—is, at its heart, a crisis of spirit, or a common ground of meaning. Highly polarized egos are incapable of recognizing that the key to wholeness lies in easing dangerous binary ways of thinking. They are blind to the values of points of view other than their own or their tribe's, and so they cannot make psychological space for common ground. In such a toxic environment, there is no possibility for what I call a communal object. Just like it sounds, a communal object is something that we all work on together. It is a cultural, collaborative project. This means that it is something in need of work and care. It needs attention because it is sick or faulty. Or perhaps it was once vital, numinous, and strong, with the power to bind people together in common purpose, but that numinosity has mysteriously vanished.

In his formulation of the transcendent function, Jung (1969d) insisted that the only way to rise out of the tension of the opposites was to allow a numinous symbol to emerge, one that could stand in as a placeholder for the new level of consciousness that had not yet arrived (p. 75). While a sign solidifies and consolidates meaning, making its contents clear to consciousness, a symbol opens and upends meaning, revealing something new (Jung, 1971, pp. 473–481). To many, America has become a sign rather than a symbol, and many have lost faith in its promise. If Haidt's positive and negative values were placed as options alongside the American flag, the most polarized among us might choose only the positive or only the negative values. But as a symbol, the wholeness of America encompasses them all: neither its shadow not its luminosity may be denied. The American dream has been a shining city on a hill for some, while remaining a hopeless mirage for many. When a symbol deteriorates into a sign, it means the ego-shadow binary has its grip on the community. The dying symbol has become a communal object, and it needs our attention. The shadow *must* be confronted and incorporated into the ego's attitude.

On one hand the crisis of spirit is a crisis of belief. We no longer have faith in our institutions because we no longer trust the motives of the individuals pulling the strings. But it is more than that. We no longer have a sense of *common* destiny or purpose. What is at stake is the myth, or divine drama, of the cultural opus. Will our work bravely face revelation, which is the new, or will it cling to the past? Jung (1969b) held that nature's work of individuation toward wholeness takes its course inevitably, just as all rivers reach the sea. Either we can be dragged along by fate, or we can be patient and reach the goal upright by taking the time to understand the messages that cross our path (p. 460). The first step in the *opus contra naturam* is to acknowledge that there are messages to be found if we dare to look through a mythic lens. By adopting a mythological perspective, we become avatars of the divine, characters in a world of story. We learn to take the author's hints, and when we do, the crisis of authority finally appears as it really is, a crisis of revelation.

In the second part of this essay, I focus on revelation as the key to rejuvenating the symbol. Just as archetypal pedagogy can help to ease the binary and restore cultural common ground, through its emphasis on fostering personal narratives an archetypal approach to self-education allows individual vocation to come forth.

Archetypal Pedagogy as an Ethical Project

For Clifford Mayes (2020) teaching and learning are life projects that necessarily involve the exploration and creation of meaningful narratives in students' lives. Such narratives are how we connect our sense of individual, biographical time, which in our modern world can often feel isolating and adrift from a sense of purpose, with Eternal Time, or the sense of the divine. In short, archetypal pedagogy seeks to "create spaces for Spirit in educational processes—public no less than private" (p. 88). For Jung (1968c), the archetype of spirit is the archetype of meaning, particularly the discovery of meaning initially hidden within the chaos of life itself (pp. 32, 35). Mayes contends that narratives are most meaningful, and therefore the most humane and the most ethical, when they are most archetypal (p. 6). In this way, archetypal pedagogy is an *opus contra naturam*, or a work against the grain of nature, which otherwise tends to blindly follow its instinctual course.

The raw, mundane events of life—what Mircea Eliade (1957) called "profane time"—seem meaningless because their connection to a larger purpose and goal is hidden from us on the level of physical, material reality. For consciousness to come to meaning, the level of the profane must somehow become connected to the higher level of the sacred. Sociologist Émile Durkheim (1965) proposed that a sense of the sacred, the foundation of all religious experience, is a way of bonding the individual to the social group (pp. 262–265). Eliade (1958) took this a step further by stating that the instinct to connect to the sacred is a vital life process that we cannot do without. Individuals and whole societies must periodically protect "against the meaningless, nothingness; to escape, in fact, from the profane sphere" (p. 33). In seeking the eternal truths of the sacred realm, "man is trying to gain salvation by uniting himself with reality" (p. 33). In existential terms, humanity must constantly reassert and reinvent itself to prevent the nihilistic drift into the oblivion of unconsciousness.

Joseph Campbell (1973), in his formulation of the hero's journey, made much the same point. A society, because of its natural inertia, tends to slip into *routine*, to use sociologist Max Weber's term (1946, pp. 245–250), and it needs the *charisma* (Weber's counterforce) of the hero, who is in touch with the gods, to complete the cycle of separation, initiation, and return so that the culture may be rejuvenated (Campbell 1973, p. 30). In Campbell's cycle there are three levels of being: the individual charismatic hero, the home society that is in danger of slipping into routine and permanent "profane time," and the sacred realm of the gods (or archetypes) that the hero must either visit or interact with to retrieve the elixir and thus restore and renew the culture. Mayes (2020), following the philosopher Paul Ricoeur, offers a similar three-level structure of time: individual biographical time, world-historical time, and eternal time (p. 35). Taking his cue from Henderson, who postulated the cultural unconscious as a middle layer between the personal and collective unconscious, Mayes sees the receptive and dialogical individual as the force that can pull the archetypes into the culture through meaningful narrative, thus redeeming world-historical time by putting it back into sync with the sacred (p. 40). World-historical culture thus becomes an *opus contra naturam* upon which the charismatic individual and the gods collaborate.

This may seem abstract and remote, but Mayes (2020) sees the threat of slippage into the meaninglessness of profane time as a very real phenomenon in today's classroom. Echoing the words of educational historian Lawrence Cremin, Mayes writes that the "military-industrial-educational complex" is now a "clear and present danger" to society:

> Colleges of education have tripped over themselves running toward ever-bigger grants to research ever-more efficient means of training teachers to train children to become obedient and efficient "worker-citizens" through the instrumentalities of standardized education—the dystopian assault on democracy through (mis)education. (p. 154)

As society sees itself more and more as a machine, its profanity transforms the individual from a thinking human being into a mere cog. The individual is denuded of her authenticity and risks suffocating conformity to the "they-self," thus obliterating any possibility for individuation.

Mayes (2020) sees a similar dynamic playing out in the world of education, making a distinction between education in "service of the sign," which is an information-based program of "social engineering" (p. 180) and leads to the conformity and regimentation (p. 171), and education in "spirit of the symbol," which is inquisitive, creative, and compassionate, a quest for wisdom upon which teacher and student embark together (p. 180). One is declarative and clings to the known while the other is interrogatory and inherently mysterious (p. 23). In Heidegger's terms, the sign is truth-as-correspondence while the symbol is truth-as-disclosure. One is not necessarily superior to the other—we need both—but to deny future growth and change, which our culture so desperately needs for its survival, is to deny the very thing that makes us human. Mayes, therefore, sees archetypal pedagogy, and the engagement with meaningful narratives, as an urgent ethical project.

Narrative, Story, and Self-Revelation

We have seen that fostering narratives is essential to connecting potentially profane and routine biographical time with the redemption of the sacred. But what, exactly, is a narrative, and what, besides connecting to archetypes, makes one meaningful? The *Oxford English Dictionary* defines *narrative* as "a spoken or written account of events; a story." A narrative, surely, could be a simple telling of events that happened, but such an account would most likely be quite boring, unless the events related to something or someone very important, and were told skillfully in such a way as to draw us in. Mayes (2020) draws upon a definition by literary theorist Robert Scholes: "A narration is the symbolic presentation of a sequence of events connected by subject matter and related by time" (cited on p. 22). This gets us a bit closer, especially with "symbolic presentation," but "events connected by subject matter and related by time" seems obvious, and such an account, absent the symbolic, could still be boring and meaningless. Clearly, then, what we really mean is *story* rather than *narrative*, and the nature of the former is that it is *symbolic*. What does this mean?

Jung (1971) thought of the symbol differently from the way most people use the term (pp. 473–481). As alluded to above, a *sign* is something that is directive, where the meaning is clear, such as a stop sign. It relates content that is already known to consciousness. Recalling Weber's terms, it is routine. A *symbol*, on the other hand, indicates something unknown to consciousness, an enigma coming from the unconscious that acts as a sort of magnet or breadcrumb that will attract psychic energy. A "living symbol" is inherently numinous to the conscious ego, because it is "pregnant with meaning" (p. 475). A symbol is charismatic because it points to the future.

The dictionary definition of *narrative* bundles together the routine "telling of events" and the richer term "story." The ancient Greeks were more nuanced: Logos is an *objective* saying or account, while Mythos is a *subjective* telling of a story that involves mortal, heroic, and divine characters. Story, then, is intimately connected to such characters and their values. Not only that, a good story, much like a symbol, draws us in and attracts our energy. We are drawn to the most powerful stories, the most *archetypal* stories, because we intuitively sense that we can learn something from them.

They tell us who we are and how to draw meaning from the raw events of life. They teach us how to go beyond simple narration, the Logos of our lives, by providing models for how to create new myths for ourselves. And one of the functions of myth, Campbell (1983) tells us, is *cosmological* (pp. 8–9). A cosmos is an ordering system, a meaningful *gestalt*, in which we find our place in a universe that is otherwise blind. If story leads to myth, and myth to cosmos, then creating a compelling story through which we act is a vital means by which the ego understands the Self. Cultural world-historical time, the realm of Henderson's cultural unconscious, is the "story world" in which we enact this drama of individuation.

Neither the symbol, nor the archetypal story for that matter, exist solely for the purpose of drawing our attention, however. A flat, action-packed story may be entertaining (to some), but it is not nourishing or fulfilling. A symbol, as well as a powerful story, always guides consciousness to a new state of awareness, but this change, or synthesis, may only be achieved by first bringing together highly charged opposites—thesis and antithesis—so that the conscious ego fully identifies with neither. As mentioned above, Jung (1971) called this process "the transcendent function":

> From the activity of the unconscious there now emerges a new content, constellated by thesis and antithesis in equal measure and standing in a *compensatory* relation to both. It thus forms the middle ground on which the opposites can be united. (p. 479, emphasis in original)

By transcendent, he does not mean "metaphysical," but *spiritual*. This is the psychic mechanism by which we come to know meaning in our lives. It is the way all individuals and cultures come to know who they are. A symbol operates at the level of the individual, while a story operates at the level of a society. A myth, being the most archetypal and potentially the most epic in scope, operates at the level of a culture or even a civilization.

Mayes (2020) comes closest to the essence of story, rather than narrative, in his discussion of Existentialist theologian Reinhold Niebhur. One should not look for "the children of light and the children of darkness" in a literal end-of-time scenario, with one side victorious over the other; rather, one should look for good and evil within oneself. "The truest narratives are apocalypses of self-recognition," writes Mayes (p. 66). With our Western, black-and-white glasses, we tend to take *apocalypse* as "the end of the world," but it actually means *uncovering, disclosure*, or *revelation*. In this sense, it is synonymous with Heidegger's *aletheia* (truth-as-disclosure) and Jung's transcendent function. It is Mythos, which opens up, rather than Logos, which stabilizes (Rowland, 2010, p. 84). Mythos creates a cosmos of communion and vocation; Logos requires distance, separation, and objectivity, generating a binding, routine system of atomized selfhoods. These two conflicting aspects of truth (Heidegger's disclosure and correspondence) form the respiration cycle of the Self. Following Jung's (1969a) elaboration of Goethe's metaphor, Mythos and Logos are the diastole and systole of the beating heart, two phases of consciousness in its desire to know and understand itself (p. 37). While Mythos ultimately brings revelation, it cannot do this without the limiting contraction of Logos.

For story analyst John Truby (2007), "self-revelation" is in fact the most important element in a series of seven key components that all stories must contain. These keys are (1) Weakness and need, (2) Desire, (3) Opponent, (4) Plan, (5) Battle, (6) Self-revelation, and (7) New equilibrium. The self-revelation is inextricably bound to the weakness and need of the protagonist. For Truby, this weakness may be merely psychological, relating only to the hero, or moral, which relates to others. In Jungian terms, we may say that a psychological weakness pertains to the personal shadow, a part of oneself perceived by the ego to be inferior or other, while a moral weakness pertains to cultural shadow, that is, values that the ego initially believes to be wrong. Importantly, this weakness remains in the protagonist's unconscious until the end of the story. Consciously, for both protagonist and audience, the desire is for a certain goal, which may or may not be achieved. But the true boon is the self-revelation, which allows the protagonist, and the audience, to arrive at a new level of consciousness. In describing the self-revelation, Truby writes, "The battle is *an intense and painful experience* for the hero. This crucible of battle causes the hero to have a major revelation about who he really is" (p. 49, emphasis mine).

The "apocalypse of self-recognition" may not be the end of *the* world, but it is surely the end of the *ego's* world. As Jung (1968b) said, "the presumption of the ego can only be damped down by moral defeat" (p. 25). What makes a story meaningful has to do with our spiritual education and our newfound capacity to grow and change, both at the biographical and cultural levels. A story is always precipitated by a catalyst, or what Truby (2007) calls a "problem," which is bound up with the weakness and need of the protagonist, or ego (p. 42). A story, then, always begins with a crisis of spirit, the necessary precursor to individual or cultural self-revelation and psychological maturation. Story, especially myth, is the native habitat for discovery and revelation. Myths model liminal periods of crisis and intense change on an epic scale. They teach us how such crises were handled (or mishandled) in the past, so that we may learn how to successfully navigate an ever-changing world. Like dreams, mythic stories prepare us to face new challenges head-on by showing us what is possible rather than what simply is. Through the grammar of archetypes and conflicting moral values, myths are demonstrations of how communal objects may be revitalized and reinvested with hope and meaning.

CONCLUSION

Readers familiar with Jungian psychology will recognize that the two-step prescription of first easing the binary and then rejuvenating the symbol is not at all new. In fact, it provides the very foundation for Jung's therapeutic approach. One first must confront the shadow, especially the personal unconscious, and only then will the soul, or anima, guide the individual to the archetypes of the collective unconscious. That transpersonal realm is where true meaning is not found as much as created, a collaborative opus between self, society, and the sacred. In the wake of World War II, Erich Neumann identified and clarified the first step with *Depth Psychology and a New Ethic* (1990), recognizing that morally elevating the ego also meant projecting shadow onto the scapegoat. As for the second step, throughout his career Jung emphasized that psychic energy was not, as Freud theorized, exclusively sexual, but that it instinctually pursues whatever gradient the totality of the psyche demands. Modern life greedily hoards that energy, affecting the persona, or the outer face of the ego, while the soul, or inner face, is left to wither away before it emerges from the unconscious as "dark and menacing." Jung recognized that psychic energy must be redirected to more positive and constructive pursuits. The spontaneously emerging symbol, produced by the unconscious, is the vessel which holds the inputs from both conscious and unconscious aspects of the psyche. We need new symbols because we need new guides for future investments of psychic energy.

What is new in our age are the obvious effects that technology, particularly social media, have had on the collective psyche. Throughout history, technology has had both positive and negative effects, but little attention has been paid to how those costs and benefits have been distributed. Technology has undoubtedly led to material progress while we have regressed spiritually; not only has it disenchanted our world, but it has led us to believe that meaning is in fact nonexistent. If there is any silver lining to this dark age we are entering, it is the revelation of the crisis of spirit itself. By eroding a sense of truth, common ground, and purpose, technology itself reveals the need to restore the meaningful ground to make our world into a cosmos. Technology also reveals its corrosive effects: the other is dehumanized, and all organic life, which is the basis of civilization, is separated and abstracted to the point of exploitation and exhaustion. There will be no progress on the first of our prescriptions until enough individuals confront these shadows in their lives. I believe little progress has been made on this front because a positive alternative has been denied to most people by the profane tendencies of material capitalist culture. To put it simply, most people are bored, and their psychic energy flows into the easiest and most immediately gratifying channels. The culture has not provided numinous myths capable of redirecting this energy into constructive pursuits.

This is where archetypal pedagogy can be a positive influence in the lives of students today, by providing an alternative to the routine, profane, and disenchanted culture of materialism. Jungian analysis and therapy are, of course, not appropriate in the classroom. So, what are the practical steps that teachers can take to offer the benefits of a Jungian approach? First, have frank and honest discussions with students about the effects of technology in their lives. How does this world make them feel? What can individuals do of their own accord to mitigate these negative effects? At the same time, the positive aspects of today's technology must be acknowledged and honored. A more sophisticated and nuanced form of thinking will naturally result. Second, facilitate open discussions about values, and learn to recognize how stories are really about the clash of values. Third, encourage students to take personality tests, as many different types as possible, to understand their own psychic orientations. Encourage them to take Haidt's moral foundations tests and link the results to personality but also question his assumptions with an eye toward cultural biases and blind spots, especially regarding marginalized values. Further, connect all the dots by providing an education in archetypes, which form the foundation for both personality and values. Finally, and most important, encourage students to actively engage with their newfound archetypal grammar by creating their own stories. Archetypes are like the keys of the piano. They are there to be played, and it is up to us to put them to work in the service of beautiful, meaningful music.

For thousands of years prophets, artists, and storytellers have warned against impending doom if our profane collective impulses are not checked. *The Course of Empire* has haunted me for decades, and those with even an inkling of an ecological education have been more than frustrated by the inability to stop a clear and present danger that has been well understood since the early 1970s. What has not been well understood is that this problem is only superficially ecological, and that the underlying disease is spiritual. I certainly did not understand that before my study of Jung. Perhaps Heidegger (2009) was right, that "only a god can still save us" (p. 326) and that "the essence of technology is not something that humans can master by themselves" (p. 324). The twentieth century produced the psychology of Jung and the philosophy of Heidegger, but it also produced some of the most profound and popular myths for the modern age: *The Lord of the Rings, Star Wars, Harry Potter,* and *A Song of Ice and Fire*. In each of those stories the characters are powerless to stop the darkness that engulfs their worlds. In each of these myths, heroes and heroines battle villains who embody the living dead. The battle is for life, and for the hope that life will persist, no matter the enemy. Their humanity is revealed not through averting the crisis but through a collective suffering that imparts wisdom for the ages: that none of us can do it alone. If anything, archetypes teach us that.

REFERENCES

Campbell, J. (1973). *The hero with a thousand faces.* Princeton University Press. (Original work published 1949)

Campbell, J. (1983). *Historical atlas of world mythology, volume 1: The way of the animal powers.* Harper & Row.

Cole, T. (1836). *The course of empire.* [Oil on canvas]. The New York Historical Society.

Coupe, L. (2005). *Kenneth Burke on myth: An introduction.* Routledge.

Durkheim, E. (1965). *The elementary forms of religious life* (J. W. Swain, Trans.). The Free Press. (Original work published 1915)

Eagleman, D. (2015). *The brain: The story of you.* Vintage Books.

Eliade, M. (1957). *The sacred and the profane: The nature of religion* (W. Trask, Trans.). Harcourt.

Haidt, J. (2012). *The righteous mind: Why good people are divided by politics and religion.* Vintage Books.

Heidegger, M. (1971). The origin of the work of art (A. Hofstadter, Trans.). In *Poetry, language, thought.* HarperCollins.

Heidegger, M. (2008). *Being and time* (J. Macquarrie & E. Robinson, Trans.).Harper & Row. (Original work published 1927)

Heidegger, M. (2009). *Der Spiegel* interview with Martin Heidegger. In G. Figal (Ed.), *The Heidegger reader* (J. Veith, Trans.). Indiana University Press.

Henderson, J. (1990). *Shadow and self: Selected papers in analytical psychology.* Chiron Publications.

Hillman, J. (1975). *Revisioning psychology.* Harper.

Hyde, L. (2010). *Trickster makes this world: Mischief, myth, and art.* Farrar, Straus and Giroux.

Jung, C. G. (1966). On the relation of analytical psychology to poetry (R. F. C. Hull, Trans.). In H. Read et al. (Eds.), *The collected works of C. G. Jung* (Vol. 15, pp. 65–83). Princeton University Press. (Original work published 1922)

Jung, C. G. (1968a). Introduction to the religious and psychological problems of alchemy (R. F. C. Hull, Trans.). In H. Read et al. (Eds.), *The collected works of C. G. Jung* (Vol. 12, 2nd ed., pp. 1–38). Princeton University Press. (Original work published 1943)

Jung, C. G. (1968b). *Aion: Researches into the phenomenology of the self* (R. F. C. Hull, Trans.) (H. Read et al., Eds.), *The collected works of C. G. Jung* (Vol. 09ii, 2nd ed.). Princeton University Press. (Original work published 1951)

Jung, C. G. (1968c). Archetypes of the collective unconscious (R. F. C. Hull, Trans.). In H. Read et al. (Eds.), *The collected works of C. G. Jung* (Vol. 9 pt. 1, 2nd ed., pp. 3–41). Princeton University Press. (Original work published 1954)

Jung, C. G. (1969a). On psychic energy (R. F. C. Hull, Trans.). In H. Read et al. (Eds.), *The collected works of C. G. Jung* (Vol. 8, 2nd ed., pp. 3–66). Princeton University Press. (Original work published 1928)

Jung, C. G. (1969b). Answer to Job (R. F. C. Hull, Trans.). In H. Read et al. (Eds.), *The collected works of C. G. Jung* (Vol. 11, 2nd ed., pp. 355–470). Princeton University Press. (Original work published 1952)

Jung, C. G. (1969c). On the nature of the psyche (R. F. C. Hull, Trans.). In H. Read et al. (Eds.), *The collected works of C. G. Jung* (Vol. 8, 2nd ed., pp. 159–234). Princeton University Press. (Original work published 1954)

Jung, C. G. (1969d). The transcendent function (R. F. C. Hull, Trans.). In H. Read et al. (Eds.), *The collected works of C. G. Jung* (Vol. 8, 2nd ed., pp. 67–91). Princeton University Press. (Original work published 1958)

Jung, C. G. (1970a). The undiscovered self (R. F. C. Hull, Trans.). In H. Read et al. (Eds.), *The collected works of C. G. Jung* (Vol. 10, 2nd ed., pp. 244–305). Princeton University Press. (Original work published 1957)

Jung, C. G. (1970b). Flying saucers: A modern myth of things seen in the skies (R. F. C. Hull, Trans.). In H. Read et al. (Eds.), *The collected works of C. G. Jung* (Vol. 10, 2nd ed., pp. 308–443). Princeton University Press. (Original work published 1958)

Jung, C. G. (1971). *Psychological types* (R. F. C. Hull, Trans.) In H. Read et al. (Eds.), *The collected works of C. G. Jung* (Vol. 6). Princeton University Press. (Original work published 1921)

Mayes, C. (2017). *Teaching and learning for wholeness: The role of archetypes in educational processes*. Roman & Littlefield.

Mayes, C. (2020). *Archetypes, culture, and the individual in education: Three pedagogical narratives*. Routledge.

Neumann, E. (1990). *Depth psychology and a new ethic* (E. Rolfe, Trans.). Shambhala. (Original work published 1949)

Rowland, S. (2010). *C.G. Jung in the humanities: Taking the soul's path*. Spring Journal Books.

Truby, J. (2007). *The anatomy of story: 22 steps to becoming a master storyteller*. Farrar, Straus and Giroux.

Weber, M. (1946). *From Max Weber: Essays in sociology* (H. H. Gerth & C. W. Mills, Eds. & Trans.). Oxford University Press.

Chapter 2

Naturally Unnatural

A Jungian Approach to Holistic Dog Training

Alexa Gallo

It is time for a shift in perspective when it comes to ideas and practices of "dog training" in the modern world. When we integrate ideas of ecopsychology with holistic dog training practices we can transform our approach from the traditional one-sided view of the superior human training the inferior dog to a shared pedagogy honoring both canine and human ways of knowing. Applying this new, expanded consciousness to training requires an archetypal shift in perception to alchemy, there is opportunity for transformation in both inner and outer realms of the psyche.

When we adopt an ecopsychological perspective, co-training with a dog becomes sacred soul work. In my own life, I've noticed a kind of morphic resonance when it comes to training my puppy Jasper. He seems to represent spirit, while I am the ego, and when we relate (via training) soul emerges in the relationship. Co-training is collaborative and the end result benefits dog, human, and perhaps most importantly, the living cosmic relationship between them. This process has invited me to question whether training a dog is natural or unnatural? Like digging up a buried bone in the yard, I'm hoping to uncover a shared epistemology between two unique disciplines: dog training and depth psychology. I believe by working with these sacred bones, we step toward a bigger shift in awareness with far reaching significance. Perhaps this "bone" is a different kind of "fossil fuel."

DOG

Shared History and Mythology

Our relationship to dogs is ancient and mysterious. There is evidence dating back to the Ice Age of humans and dogs living in symbiotic relationship with each other (Woloy, 2018, p. 7). Humans were communicating with dogs before written language or known glyphs. We shared an instinctive language of image, feeling, and intuition. Our ability to communicate with dogs reveals a significant connection between us. Theologian Martin Buber said, "An animal's eyes have the power to speak a great language" (1923/2000, p. 73). He is putting into words the intuitive knowing we have when we gaze into our dog's eyes. We can communicate without words that we are on the psychic or cosmic level *with* them. As ecopsychologist Ian McCallum says,

> [T]he aim of human to animal communication is clear. It is not about trying to get the animals to like you, or to have them at your beck and call. Instead, through body language, tone of voice, or even music, it is to let them know you mean no harm; that you want to learn not only about them, but from them. (2009, p. 185)

He is pointing out that the way we communicate with animals is through the body. We create images with our tone, body language, and sound. These "images" are understood and communicated trans-species. Part of our disconnect from the natural world is reflected in the way that most of us take this incredible truth for granted, living in the narcissistic bubble that humans are superior and disconnected from all other forms of life.

Dogs (and their ancestors, the wolf, fox, and bear) are central to nearly all indigenous ceremonies and mythologies (Woloy, 2018 p. 28). Prior to the rise of Western culture, the dog was worshipped as a god or sacred deity—from Anubis, the towering Egyptian god with the head of a jackal, the Lakota Coyote-Trickster, Greek goddess Diana and her hounds, Cerberus of the underworld, to the Fool of the Tarot with the dog nipping his heel. Up in the sky, the brightest star of all is Sirus, the dog. This particular star is central to ancient navigation and ritual (Woloy, 2018). The symbol of the dog is found at gateways and thresholds and is known as a guide to souls after death (Woloy, 2019, pp. 35–38).

The Fall

There is an archetypal connection between dogs and humans. Woloy (2019) connects the special relationship of the Earth Goddess and her companion dog (p. xi). She found this sacred pairing in most all cultures. In other words, the sacred feminine aspect of the psyche naturally relates to animal instinct, in particular, the dog. Thus, "the dog is part of feminine mystery" (Woloy, 2018, p. xii). Parallel to the fall of the goddess culture, so too the dog has fallen from grace. Woloy aptly points out the different slang. "She's a dog" means that she is ugly or worthless. "To go to the dogs" is to deteriorate, degenerate, or go to ruin. To "lead a dog's life" is to be unhappy or pathetic (2018, p. 67). When we hear the word "bitch," we hear a curse, we don't conjure the image of a mother dog suckling her pups.

It is significant that the dog fell from status *as* Judeo-Christian values rose to prominence. The dog is rarely mentioned in *The Bible*, and when it is, it is associated with the devil, being unclean and lowly (Woloy, 2018, p. 66). Woloy uses this information to support her claim of the archetypal relationship between the dog and the feminine. They fell from grace together. The new patriarchal worldview was ruled by rationality, empirical thinking, and causality. The body was not to be trusted, and neither was the feminine, least of all the dog. Many ecopsychologists link this shift to our current environmental crisis. When we rejected the goddess and the dog, we rejected all of nature.

I believe, along with St. Teresa of Lisieux, the "Little Saint," that the little things are the big things. Clearly we have been living in the nigredo, the shadow of the dog and the goddess. And now there are glimmerings and stirrings. The old bone is ready to be dug up. Perhaps now it is time to emerge with something both ancient and new. As we are invited to heal and "train" our relationship to dogs, we are also invited to heal our relation to nature and the feminine as well.

Canine Renaissance

Dogs are now the most popular pet in the United States. During the 2020–2021 COVID-19 pandemic, dog adoptions increased by 40% and the animal shelters had waiting lists (Hedgpeth, 2021). Prior to COVID-19, Americans were already outspending themselves each year on their pets, and again that number soared during the pandemic (DeCiccio, 2020). People are commissioning portraits, buying organic dog popsicles, and on any given day in New York City you are likely to see someone pushing their beloved pooch in a baby carriage, maybe wearing a cashmere sweater with painted pink nails. Dogs are regaining royal status. It is a time of renaissance and alchemy for the dog and the families who adopt them.

ECOPSYCHOLOGICAL PERSPECTIVES

Alchemy and Transformation

Woloy states that "the wisdom of the Goddess carries with it the deep wisdom of connection to otherness in the form of the instinctive side of ourselves" (2018, p. 69). She also quotes Jungian Barbara Hannah describing the dog instinct as "deep instinct to do what is just right, at just the right moment" (2018, p. 51). Global temperatures are rising, heat is building, there is division and great collective rage. We truly are within the crucible. Alchemy reminds us that working with the poison brings the medicine. It is healing to witness the return of the goddess and return of the dog to her side.

Alchemy is personal and collective. Alternative medicine, alternative facts, quantum physics, and holistic dog training are wildly different topics, yet they are all pointing in the same direction. We are navigating rough seas, and the old maps no longer apply. It is time to look up at the stars, time to look into the eyes of our dogs, time to feel into the wisdom contained within our bodies and trust that there are other ways of knowing that are equally valid and completely different from the dominating anthropocentric point of view. This represents a move away from scientific reason but not a total abandonment of it, for it has produced enormous good as well as enormous bad. *Biocentric* anthropomorphism identifies and honors the commonalities between species using human language to communicate what we respectfully observe (Hayen, 2017, p. 174). Ralph Metzner describes the movement out of postmodernism into the ecological age as a natural, evolutionary shift (2006, p. 93).

As a symbolic gatekeeper and guide of souls, the dog is uniquely situated in both our outer world, as pet, and inner world, as archetypal guide. According to ecopsychology, what happens outside is a reflection of inner processes that can render those unique processes to the conscious mind primarily through symbols because of their high semantic valence. We are deeply impacted by not only our personal history but by our community and ecosystem. We are not separate, but rather part of everything. Dr. Lisa Strom writes that when a person is transformed, there is "no going back to the previous way of living or being" (2015, p. 10). She and Woloy go on to describe the various ways dogs can aid in human transformation as potential healers, from the licking the tears of an emotional wound, to placing their head on the chest of someone with a broken heart; they also can awaken words and communication from people with autism and dementia (Strom, 2015, pp. 31–36; Woloy, 2018, pp. 32–33).

Training Is "Unnatural"

"To know ourselves we have to know our own animal nature first" (McCallum, 2009, p. 175). Our animal nature is natural. Our human nature is natural. How did we come to this idea of "unnatural"? I have heard it said that when humans use consciousness to create, the result is unnatural. I cannot recall where I heard this, but it intuitively felt true in my heart. For example, when humans began to control breeding of animals, they transformed from wild to domestic (Woloy, 2018, p. 7). When we build a structure, if we use items found in nature, like rocks, mud, and stone, it feels more natural than the construction of a building of fiberglass, plastic, and metal. This is just intuitive. We know what natural means; we can feel it in our bones.

Thus it follows that training an animal is unnatural for both the dog and the human. In this "unnatural" process we find a shared understanding.

Jung never minimized the colossal collective scope of this work, nor did he sugarcoat what it would cost the individual—at least a critical mass of them—to purposefully evolve psychospiritually. This would, he said, be an *opus contra naturam*, "a work against nature." Training means learning something new. It is both a source of frustration/shadow and also a place to connect and create something new. Co-training is an alchemical process. Traditional dog training is more one-sided, with the "superior" human controlling "primitive" animal. But is this really true? From an ecopsychological perspective, both creatures are offering and inviting each other. The human may hold the "treat," the material that symbolizes the reward, but the dog is in control of its behavior. It "treats" the human by learning and agreeing to perform the command. It is a choice; the dog is not a machine to be programmed. Both animals are using free will, a system of reward, and finding a way to communicate across species lines. This is highly unnatural for each. Or is it?

Perhaps the paradox of being human is that we have the unique capacity to be "unnatural." The birth of consciousness brought with it the confusion over our identity and center. With consciousness, we became aware that we are both unique individuals and yet connected to a greater whole. We are the one and the sum. It is a paradoxical situation that has led us into some very destructive behavior, especially when we confuse ourselves with the totality. I believe one of the reasons we are seeing a rise in narcissistic personality disorder in parallel with the destruction of environment is due to this confusion. Humans suffering from narcissism only see themselves; they are blind to the *other* forms of beauty around them.

According to Jungian psychology, individuation is the alchemical transformation in awareness from ego-center to Self-center. By making this shift, we engage the archetypes and the imaginal, sacred realm of inner knowing. If being "unnatural" is our natural state, then when we engage in small actions, such as co-training a dog, we can begin to encourage a more conscious relationship to ourselves and unconscious realms that both frighten and beckon us. To clarify, our "unnatural" state is one of human creativity, invention, and utility. So it is natural for us to be unnatural. The very act of merging conscious awareness with unconscious symbols is fertile ground; it is Psyche and Eros. It is in our nature to create, and if we do not honor the mystery that drives us, we become lost in our egos. From this neurotic place, if we are lucky, we might find a dog to help guide us back to our animal nature.

To confront our natural, inner animal requires courage, a willingness to be disturbed, "to enter the wild places of Earth and the wild psyche at the same time" (McCallum, 2009, p. 175). McCallum says that we will need a guide, and I would suggest what better guide than a dog? Dogs are the guardians and gatekeepers. While I am not comparing dog training to shamanic practice, I would say that I agree with Mircea Eliade (1964/1992) who said "we are in dire need of modern day specialists in the sacred" (p. 176). There seems to be a general call to bring the sacred forth into the everyday, and thus the ordinary becomes sacred, and we begin the process of soul-making as James Hillman describes the process of recovering the alienated soul (1977, p. 78).

Ecopsychologist Jeffrey Kiehl echoes this sentiment when he describes envisioning new and creative ways forward to address the climate crisis, asking us to "be conscious of what images, patterns, or metaphors could activate transformation" (Kiehl, 2016, pp. 55–56). Even more significant, he asks us to look in unexpected places for the solution, to the nonessential, the knowing of the body and the heart (p. 10). Depth psychologists have paid attention to dreams, art, and creativity. Why not shift our gaze in another direction and meet our dogs nose-to-nose as co-trainers and soul makers?

Mitakuyé Oyasin

There is a Lakota prayer *"Mitakuyé Oyasin!"* which means "For All My Relations!" It is used as a greeting, an introduction, and an invitation to deepen into a relationship with the most sacred energy of all: Wakan Tanka, the Creator, the Great Mystery. When we say "For All My Relations" we are honoring the Earth and all parts as family, as relations. There are the Standing Nation (the plants), the Winged Ones (the birds), and the Four-Legged Nation, (animals). *Mitakuyé Oyasin* represents an inherent trust and connection to all aspects of nature (Wahpepah, 2018). Jungian analyst Jerome Bernstein refers to this perspective as "reciprocity psyche" (2018, p. 18). Meanwhile, Western consciousness is "dominion psyche." Dominion psyche is logical, binary, and "crushes the spirit dimension" (p. 24). A wonderful *apologia* for a hermeneutics of nature.

According to Bernstein, as Western consciousness evolves, it is moving toward "borderland consciousness," which includes a dialogue between indigenous reciprocity psyche and the "old" dominion psyche (Bernstein, 2018, p.18). I believe that Melissa Jackson's holistic approach to dog training (Jackson, 2020a) provides one method of connecting with borderland consciousness in everyday life.

But the inner processes—upon which the arithmetic procedures finally rest—are quite different and generally sovereign process; and they wither and die if conditions do not support them. Bernstein warns that if we continue with solely a dominion psyche, we will not redeem the spirit dimension and our species is at risk for extinction (along with the rest of the planet, p. 26).

McCallum gives us a modern reminder that "how we care for animals and place is a reflection for how we care for ourselves and each other" (2009, p. 173). He goes on to say that "when we are compelled to act by emotion, the situation is archetypal . . . any step towards helping animals or the environment is connected to our deep sense of wanting to help ourselves" (McCallum, 2009). In other words, when we "train" our dogs, we are also "training" ourselves. Jung describes the process of individuation as the center of the psyche shifting from ego-orientation to Self-orientation. Individuation is a holistic move that requires the ego to humble itself and recognize that it is not the center. It has been called an "educative act," the specific venues and ethical of which play out in ever unique moments of individually rich and unique instances of existential encounter with each other. In these moments of "I-Thou" speech and action 1965), one alternately teaches to and learns from the other in moments of ethical encounter that are quintessentially pedagogical. The moments of Encounter carry both promise and peril as both dialogical partners come to dwell together in the tent of ever unfolding, ever emerging acts of revelation in educative encounter, one after another in one great educative act that is our life itself.

There is a sharp distinction to be drawn between these educative acts in all their specificity, interest, and risk, on one hand, and what Mayes calls "educational processes," on the other hand, in which students follow a generally state-determined curriculum that is presented in a standardized fashion for predetermined instrumental purposes that cater to the needs (and often enough, the demands) of the increasingly total state. America's greatest educational historian, Lawrence Cremin, called this, in his last and crowning study, the massive 3,000-page tome *American Education*, "the military-industrial-*educational* complex. At the end of the 20th century, Cremin reckoned that this complex would be the single greatest threat to American democracy in the 21st (Cremin, 1988). Alas, he has proven correct as more and more students feel that their creativity is being crucified on the pallid cross of a sterile empiricism.

On the other hand (or other paw), dogs symbolically represent a gateway to the unconscious, like Cerberus who stands at the gateway to the underworld; then entering a reciprocal relationship with them could mirror and enhance the individuation process itself. Perhaps helping the human become more balanced and aligned as they both give and receive lessons to the canine they are working with. Working with dogs can trigger powerful personal complexes, revealing opportunities for growth and healing for all parties.

REAL WORLD EXAMPLES: FORMS OF TRAINING

Thanks to our one-sided emphasis on so-called natural causes, *causality* [emphasis added] we have learned to differentiate what is subjective and psychic from what is objective and "natural." For primitive man, on the contrary, the psychic and the objective coalesce in the external world. (Jung, 2002, pp. 110–11)

Jung is pointing out our human propensity for one-sidedness, our desire to control and work with, operate predominately on the basis of causal relationships. He describes this as "modern" and points out that for "primitive" humans there was a balance struck between the inner and outer worlds, between causal-rational and acausal-irrational trans-rational experiences. Now, critics of Jung will jump all over the word "irrational" and accuse Jung of a sort of fantastical narcissism. But this off-center conclusion is not true, again as witnessed by three generations of brilliance in the spheres of science.

By means of the dialectal creative process, which Jung called the transcendent function, Jung was always aiming at truth that *embraces but transcends* simple binaries such as true/false, unyielding and stern rationalism, on one hand, and the fluffy gullibility of a Pollyannaism, on the other hand. This dichotomy, this transcendent function, powered by the twin engines of mind and spirit, should, Mayes insists (2020) come to saturate the student both epistemologically at the heuristic level. One should always make that distinction clear when using Jung's very unfortunate use of the term *irrational*, which is similar to Bernstein's description of the reciprocity psyche (Bernstein, 2018, p.18). Throughout Jung's work he describes the dangers of one-sided thinking that leads to complexes, neuroses, and even psychoses if left unbalanced. Traditional forms of dog training are based on behavior, cause and effect. They do not honor the acausal, spiritual, and mysterious nature of the dog (and ourselves).

During this past year of the pandemic, dog adoption rates soared. In my own life, I lost my mother to pancreatic cancer just as the COVID crisis was beginning. It was almost exactly one year ago today that she died. As I was experiencing layers of grief, both personal and collective, we (my husband

and I), like so many of the stunned and terrified human nation, decided to adopt a fur-baby of our own. A small, sparkling, fluffball from a ranch in Montana, Jasper, the mini–Australian Shepherd, found his new home with us and everyone involved and was transformed forever.

Having failed to train my beloved first dog, Hendrix, I had a nagging sense that I was "missing something." When Hendrix was small, I brought him to a local dog trainer who informed me that he was "untrainable," due to his lack of food-drive, hound-ancestry, and generally stubborn attitude. Hendrix is now a well-loved, totally untrained, senior dog. I could sense that we had a "missed connection," and I longed to have a closer, more reciprocal relationship with Jasper. I didn't realize at the time when Hendrix was young that I needed training just as much as he did.

Several synchronicities led me to Jasper and then to Melissa Jackson (2020). She writes, "Dog training isn't just about training the dog, it is learning what dogs are telling us, what we are telling our dogs, and how we can be in harmony as a pack" (Jackson, 2020). Her training ethos intuitively embodies the principles of ecopsychology and reveals the hidden, shared epistemology between them.

Melissa abruptly changed career paths after her own transformative experience of being saved from trauma by a normally timid dog, who fiercely defended her while out for a run. The dog who came to her defense was running loose, having somehow separated from its owner, and Melissa had never met the dog before. But when this dog witnessed the attack, like any protective guardian to a goddess, he naturally leaped to her aid and fiercely chased away the aggressor. The dog later returned to her side, both of them shaking. According to his owner, this dog normally cowers in fear when meeting new people, especially males. Both Melissa and the dog were transformed in this symbolic initiation. She went on to quit her job and founded Juniper Trails based on this shared experience of honor, respect, and healing.

I will now explore three of Melissa's personal favorite training techniques ("wander," "target," and "find your purpose") from an archetypal lens. By working on an archetypal level, I hope to reveal how her applied methods relate to ecopsychology, individuation, and soul-making.

Wander

The purpose of the wandering training exercise is to teach the dog to pay attention to you. The trick is that you are also paying close attention to them. In Jungian terms, paying attention is significant. It is where we begin to step into the role of the witness, the nonjudgmental observer. Wander is one of the precursors to walking loosely with a leash, or walking together, as a pack, without a leash. It leads to a sense of community, trust, and respect.

The exercise involves an open space, a long leash, and a few treats. When the pup is introduced to the new place, they are distracted and interested in everything. As they run in one direction, you walk briskly in the opposite direction; as soon as they switch directions, you also pivot and switch, but opposite to your dog. Eventually they notice, and they run over, making eye contact, which is their way of asking to be invited to "pack up" (Jackson, 2021), or join your pack. When they do this, you drop a treat and give lots of praise. It is interesting to note that the move is paradoxical. By turning away, you invite their curiosity to approach. Having the ability to work with paradox is one of the key elements in the individuation process. As I worked on "wandering," I was able to bring conscious action and feel a little deeper into the process of integrating ego and Self.

Wander is also an exercise of alignment. As I practice with Jasper, my ego is triggered. I am afraid that he isn't connecting with me; he isn't paying attention. Maybe something is wrong with him. Or worse, am I projecting? Is something wrong with me? I have often felt the hermit is one of the archetypes at my core identity. The hermit can invite inward focus and attention, but it can also alienate and withdraw. I often struggle with the shadow of the hermit in my daily life. As an introvert, it's hard for me to connect with others, and especially I struggle with intimate relationships. While we wander, I am working through these thoughts, some conscious, some unconscious. Shadow material is being unearthed, and when we finally "pack up" together, it is the best feeling! We are united; we are one pack. It is totally unnatural, human and canine, and yet, the most natural thing we could do.

Target

Similar to "wander," target is about directing attention. In this case, it is about finding a shared focus. The goal of the training is to direct your attention toward an object and for the dog to quickly touch it with their nose. There are broad applications once a dog knows how to target (Jackson, 2020a). Most important, it gives them a sense of confidence and purpose. It is a stepping-stone to teach dogs to close doors, turn off lights, and keep focus in distracting situations.

You teach the dog to first focus on a close-by object, I used the lid of a Tupperware container. When Jasper sniffs the target, touches it directly with his nose, he gets a treat—and so on. He quickly learned to read my body language, and now, if I direct my attention to any object and say "Target!" he will run over and make contact. I have used this in situations where I need him to pay attention or shift away from an aggressive dog.

From a psychological perspective, "target" is like a psychic "packing up." In other words, it gives me the same feeling as if we were walking together in a cohesive pack, but it is internal and invisible. I could say "target" in a crowded room, direct my attention toward an object, and Jasper would come running to touch it. I don't view it as a command but an invitation. Jasper wants to connect as much as I do, which is why we are successful. It reminds me of Rupert Sheldrake's writing on morphic resonance, which describes the patterns of formative causation that underlie reality (Combs & Holland, 2000, p. 24). In other words, when Jasper and I both work on "targeting," we are engaging in similar patterns of behavior, which are held within the morphic field. We understand each other because we share similar patterns. This is also congruent with Jung's ideas of archetypes as universal patterns shared between people (Combs & Holland, 2000).

Purpose

According to Jackson, "purpose is what your dog lives for. It's what drives, motivates, and makes them feel fulfilled . . . as it is the essence of who they are. But it is our responsibility to help cultivate that purpose and give them jobs that fulfill that need" (Jackson, 2020a, p. 2). She goes on to warn that if don't help them find their purpose, they will find it on their own, which might take the form of destructive behavior (Jackson, 2020a).

Similar to Jung's personality types, Jackson has identified three main types of dogs: observers, partners, and comforters. Each needs different jobs and different styles of communication. If you have adopted an observer, but you treat your dog as if their purpose was to comfort you, the dog will show signs of stress and probably have difficulty adjusting (Jackson, 2020a). All dogs have some aspect of each type, in the same way we all exhibit some qualities of both introversion and extraversion. But if we force an introvert to go to parties every night, they will quickly become neurotic. The same goes for dog type (Jackson, 2020a).

Identifying our dog's purpose requires us to put aside our ego and see the dog for who they really are (Jackson, 2020a, p. 7). For many people, this can be a difficult training exercise. It is an excellent exercise for inviting connection to the Self, for being present to what is, rather than what you want. To witness and encourage the unfolding of an "other" is deeply gratifying, as it reflects our own need to be witnessed in our unfolding. It is a gesture of respect and reverence for the present moment.

In my own life, I would like a "comfort dog." Jasper is a "partner" and Hendrix is an "observer." I have learned to accept them as they are, rather than force a projection of who I want them to be. (Luckily, I have a "comfort cat," Lefty, and perhaps he will inspire my next paper.) But the reality is that both Hendrix and Jasper provide endless comfort by being who they are meant to be. And I have found that in accepting and loving them, I learn to accept and love myself at the same time. I love watching Hendrix sniffing, observing, quietly taking in the environment around him. He teaches me to follow my nose, to watch carefully, and to take my time smelling all the good smells of life. I love the sparky energy of Jasper running in circles trying to herd Hendrix and the cats together. I love the way he feels like that kid on the sports team: "Hey, hey, hey! Put me in, Coach!" He's always ready to play. And when he plays, it 110%. He is joy personified, and he is hilariously funny.

CONCLUSION

There is not much difference between therapeutic relationships with dogs and casual relationships with them as pets except that relationships with dogs in the therapy room are, for the most part, intentional. (Hayen, 2017, p. 82)

The purpose of this paper has been to address the fact that bringing intentionality (or consciousness) to the casual dog owner while engaged in basic training can bring forth new consciousness and individuation for both dog and human, even if the dog is not a certified therapy dog. The process of individuation involves separation, differentiation, and as we separate, we also become increasingly aware of our interconnectedness. Our dogs can help us bridge this gap, as we help them with their own unique purposes. Hayen references Heidegger, pointing out that the main trouble with humans is our tendency to become trapped in the "triviality of everyday-ness" (2017, p. 150).

Jasper and Hendrix transport and transform my mundane life into an adventure. Education, guided by archetypal principles, purposes, and perspectives, can work the same magic on and for the teacher and student, where each one alternately fills each role from time to time. And when this happens, it transforms merely instrumental educational processes—which are too often a small moment in a student's life narrative—into those educative acts, which, in the presence of the dialogical Other, make us more human and humane.

REFERENCES

Bernstein, J. S. (2018). Different realities: What is reality and what difference does it make? *Psychological Perspectives, 61*(1), 18–26. https://doi.org/10.1080/00332925.2018.1422657

Buber, M. (2000). *I and thou* (1st ed.). Hesperides Press. (Original work published 1923)

Combs, A., & Holland, M. (2000). *Synchronicity: Through the eyes of science, myth and the trickster* (3rd ed.). Da Capo Press.

DeCiccio, E. (2020, December 5). The pet business is booming as Americans spend more on their animals while they work from home. CNBC. Retrieved March 22, 2021, from https://www.cnbc.com/2020/12/05/americans-are-spending-more -money-on-their-pets-during-the-pandemic.html

Eliade, M. (1992). *Shamanism archaic techniques of ecstasy*. Princeton University Press.

Hayen, C. J. (2017). *Canine-Assisted Psychotherapy: Finding the way back to our animal soul*. (10683316) [Doctoral dissertation, Pacifica Graduate Institute]. Proquest. https://search-proquest-com.pgi.idm.oclc.org/docview/1972657993 /4288DEE158254353PQ/1?accountid=45402

Hedgpeth, D. (2021, January 6). So many pets have been adopted during the pandemic that shelters are running out. *The Washington Post*. Retrieved March 22, 2021, from https://www.washingtonpost.com/dc-md-va/2021/01/06/animal -shelters-coronavirus-pandemic/

Hillman, J. (1977). *Re-visioning psychology*. Harper Perennial.

Jackson, M. (2020a). *Cultivating our dog's purpose: A workbook*. Juniper Trails Dog Training.

Jackson, M. (2020b). Home page. Juniper Trails Dog Training. Retrieved March 19, 2021, from https://www.junipertrailsdogtraining.com/

Jung, C. G. (2002). *The earth has a soul: The nature writings of C. G. Jung* (M. Sabini, Ed.). North Atlantic Books.

Kiehl, J. (2016). *Facing climate change: An integrated path to the future*. Columbia University Press.

McCallum, I. (2009). *Ecological intelligence: Rediscovering ourselves in nature*. Fulcrum Publishing.

Metzner, R. (2006). Transitions to an ecological age. *The Trumpeter, 22*(1), 89–100. Retrieved March 22, 2021, from https://trumpeter.athabascau.ca/index.php/trumpet /article/view/34/29

Strom, L. S. (2015). *From head to tale: Therapy dog training as transformative journey*. (1692034) [Doctoral dissertation, Pacifica Graduate Institute]. Proquest. https: //search-proquest-com.pgi.idm.oclc.org/

Woloy, E. (2018). *The symbol of the dog in the human psyche: A study of the human-dog bond* (Chiron monograph series). Chiron Publications. (Original work published 1990)

Chapter 3

Teaching Mysteries in the Classroom With Archetypal Pedagogy and Active Imagination

Claire T. Savage

The readers to whom this essay is dedicated are the classroom teachers who have been called to devote themselves to nurture our most vulnerable, for it is through their efforts that the youngest members of the human tribe are cared for. In the best of all possible worlds, teachers would have the resources they need to attend to academics *and* to the essence of who we are and why we are here. An article in *The Guardian* (Bekiempis, 2021) showed that the last words a student wrote before assaulting his classmates were that he felt the world was dead and his life was useless. It is my hope that the ideas discussed here may provide an antidote to such despair and a way to experience a sense of belonging so that each student can recognize their inherent value and find the strength to contribute of themselves to the building of a better world.

Educational psychologist Clifford Mayes has devoted himself to this cause and has paved the way for new generations of scholars to add to his opus. In this essay I will focus on Mayes's *Teaching Mysteries: Foundations of Spiritual Pedagogy* (2005), a small but inspiring book that classroom teachers may turn to for emotional and spiritual sustenance. Mayes's ideas are like *points of light* that illuminate the inner world and permeate outwardly beyond their visible wavelength so that students and teachers feel connected to themselves, to others, and to a sense of meaning that reaches beyond the day-to-day human realm. These points of light include the essential components of any psychospiritually informed education.

As a classroom teacher myself, I am interested in tools of practical application. In this regard, I have found that the work of depth psychologist Robert

Romanyshyn is a fine complement to that of Mayes, and in particular, the four-step process developed in his book *The Wounded Researcher: Research with Soul in Mind* (2013b). While Romanyshyn applies these steps to qualitative research methods, I will apply them here to the practice of bringing soul into the classroom. Together, Mayes and Romanyshyn create a dynamic container within which the development of soul may be awakened.

A PLACE TO CALL HOME

In these fraught and often confusing times, with rapid change on many fronts, our input as classroom teachers is needed more than ever. Students rely on us for guidance to orient themselves to the world within and around them. C. G. Jung says that we must find new ways to adapt to our ever-changing landscape: "We are living in general chaos . . . [with] confusion and disorientation and we are profoundly bewildered through this experience which we cannot put into the frame of things we have hitherto known . . . [we] must find or create a new orientation . . . a new cosmos out of the chaos" (Jung, 1933, p. 905).

Finding and creating a new orientation is precisely what Mayes does in *Teaching Mysteries*. He gives us concepts to befriend, images to inhabit, and permission to trust our deeper knowing. Ephemeral and yet concrete, Mayes provides a place for the soul to call home. The aspects of mystery that he writes about could be considered spiritual, as they are qualitatively different from the physical and the mental constructs with which we are more familiar; but they are not necessarily metaphysical, nor do they have to be associated with any one religious tradition. What's important, according to Mayes, is that student and teacher grasp something that inspires and marks their experience as meaningful.

Like religious teachings, but without the specificity of their stories of origin and the particularity of gods and goddesses, Mayes's work reconnects us to the ground of our religious instincts. This is invaluable, as religious practice has fallen away or never even existed, for it invites us to consider the deeper meaning of our lives and our feelings as human beings in a complex universe. "Religion," Jung says, "gives us a rich application for our feelings. It gives meaning to life" (Jung, 1977, p. 69).

Bridging religious sensibilities and the field of education is what Mayes has created through his theory and practice of *Archetypal Pedagogy*. Archetypes are central concepts in Jungian psychology, and through their images, they provide a foundation of psychic life and a way to connect with ancient and eternal ways of being. The image of the Great Mother for instance, could represent the womb from which we are born and the place to which we will one day return. Jung says "the totality of all archetypes is the deposit of all human experience right back to its remotest beginnings" (Jung, 1969b, p. 157). And "an archetype is, so to speak, an 'eternal' presence" (Jung, 1968, p. 221). The archetypal image of the Great Mother does not have to be limited to our biological or mortal mother, but rather, her image could represent the cyclical nature of life, death, and rebirth. Archetypal pedagogy is thus concerned with bridging educational theory and practice with "the realm of the ever-enduring" (Jung, 1966, p. 82).

Archetypal pedagogy has, I believe, two main goals: the engagement of archetypal imagery, which provides a connection to something beyond the human realm, and, to the sociocultural wish that we be kind to one another. In *Teaching Mysteries* these goals are supported by the wisdom of some of the world's most well-known spiritual teachers: Black Elk, the 19th-century Oglala Sioux medicine man; Don Juan, the modern Jacqui medicine shaman; and Martin Buber, the 20th-century theologian, among others. Mayes weaves their wisdom into his points of light that I believe can illuminate the day-to-day lives of teachers and students.

A SACRED PRECINCT

Let's begin with the sacred precinct, or as it is called in Greek, a *temenos* (Jung, 1956, 1959, 1963). A *temenos* is an alchemical word used to designate a temple in which the presence of the sacred can be felt. A *temenos* is a psychological container that describes "wherever people are passionately engaged with each other in a potentially transformative experience" (Mayes, 2016, p. 128). There are many ways teachers and students do this every day in classrooms all over the world, but the inclusion of the idea of a *temenos* can add an additional layer of meaning, for a *temenos* is more than merely symbolic, and some Jungians even make the intriguing claim that it can involve the generation of "psychophysical energies that form a quantum field which forms a fertile ground for the emergence of synchronistic phenomena" (Mayes, 2005, p. 54).

A synchronicity is when two or more events coincide in time and/or space that appear to be a-causally related, as when, for example one thinks about a friend from childhood and just then the phone rings and it is her. The two events feel meaningfully related and bear a psychological connection, but one cannot be shown to have caused the other. According to Jung, a synchronicity "consists of two factors: a) An unconscious image comes into consciousness either directly (i.e., literally) or indirectly (symbolized or suggested) in the form of a dream, idea, or premonition. b) An objective situation coincides with this content" (Jung, 1969c, pp. 441–442 and p. 447). Synchronicities in the classroom can provide teachers and students with the feeling of significance in the shared moment. "Von Franz captures something of the uniqueness of synchronistic events when she says that "they are experienced as miracles" (von Franz, 1980, pp. 78, 95, as quoted in Romanyshyn, 2013a, p. 302). A *temenos* could be considered an inner experience that gradually builds on itself to create an internal world where deeply significant events and transformative experiences can be held.

SYMBOLIC THINKING

Transformative experiences are enhanced with the use of symbols that "can accommodate many meanings, even contradictory ones, at the same time" (Mayes, 2016, p. 118). The spaciousness of symbols invites the psyche to find its own way, where imaginings, feelings, and sensations ebb and flow among the known and the unknown and draw the psyche into relationship with the wisdom of a deeper source. Symbolic thinking, cultivated in the classroom alongside other subjects, can orient students to acknowledge their inherent value and existential purpose. As Jung said, "We are badly in need of the symbolic life. Only the symbolic life can express the soul . . . and my role as one of the actors in the divine drama of life" (Jung, 1976, p. 274).

To participate in the "divine drama of life" is to feel as if we belong to something that is enduring and meaningful. The here and now is woven together with the eternal, which, when it makes its presence felt in the classroom, can lift the spirits of teacher and student alike. Mayes encourages the "use not only [of] time's direct language but also the intuitive grammar of eternity" (Mayes, 2005, p. 42), which means that a symbol can straddle both worlds, standing clear as form and figure in the everyday world and wavering as mist and inspiration in the imaginal.

Mayes says that Black Elk recounted "he would try to make words for the meaning [of his tour of the universe, but] it would be like fog and get away from [him]" (Mayes, 2005, p. 43). Chuangtse, the third century B.C.E. Taoist sage, called his experiences "teaching with doctrine with no words" (Mayes, 2005, p. 43). In the classroom, it can be helpful for teachers to understand that they may be tasked with speaking different types of languages within the same lesson. For instance, while a teacher may speak about something as tangible as the height of the Himalaya mountains, they could also be speaking about the mystery of existence itself, moving between the physical dimensions of the mountain, the cultural and religious stories of the people, and the realization that they are part of an ongoing and eternal journey.

DESTINY

Our participation in life's divine drama can be enlivened even more so by the inclusion of a sense of destiny: the necessary, fateful, and perhaps even predetermined succession of events of our existence. Jung speaks of destiny as something that gave him a feeling of security and guided him throughout his life. In *Memories, Dreams, Reflections* (1961) Jung wrote,

> From the beginning I had a sense of destiny, as though my life was assigned to me by fate and had to be fulfilled. This gave me an inner security, and although I could never prove it to myself, it proved itself to me. I did not have the certainty, it had me. (48)

It could be thought that we live within the bounds of our own destiny—as Plato suggested in the Myth of Er. Plato personified destiny as the three daughters of the Goddess of Necessity, known collectively as the Fates. In the mythical world when the soul arrives from a previous life it is required to stand before the Fates whose job it is to determine, to ratify, and then to secure the soul's journey in its next incarnation.

The first Fate is named Lachesis, which means "disposer of lots, or to obtain by fate." Lachesis measures and apportions the length of the thread of one's life. Her duty is to fulfill the soul's choices and to serve as its eternal guardian. She then leads the soul to the second of the three personifications of destiny: Clotho, whose name means "to twist by spinning." Her function is to weave one's lot and destiny into a unified whole. Clotho then leads the soul to the third and final Fate, Atropos, whose name means "inflexible," and who secures one's life into an irreversible destiny.

And then, just before the soul is to be birthed into human form, and without a backward glance, it passes through the Plain of Lethe, the plain of forgetting, so upon arrival into this world, the memory of all previous activities will have dropped away. But while the details of the story will have been forgotten, the inescapable pattern of one's life will remain intact. It exists in the background of consciousness and often takes a lifetime to comprehend—but its small, still voice is our constant companion.

The concept of destiny may provide a sense of continuity that weaves together the past, the present, and the future, and it can give the soul a place to feel as if it belongs in the cosmic order. In these often-troubling times, a sense of destiny can ease a worried mind with reassurance that on a very deep level, all is exactly as it should be. Jung (1961) spoke of how destiny alleviated his own suffering:

It was only after the illness that I understood how important it is to affirm one's destiny. In this way we forge an ego that does not break down when incomprehensible things happen: an ego that endures, that endures the truth, and that is capable of coping with the world and with fate. Then, to experience defeat is also to experience victory. Nothing is disturbed—neither inwardly nor outwardly—for one's own continuity has withstood the current of life and of time. (Jung, 1961, p. 297)

Might it be possible that the way our lives have unfolded was meant to be? Does the notion of destiny carry with it the blessings of decisions made before our birth? Does an acquiescence to our role in life's divine drama soften the heart and carry us along the current of an eternal river? Questions to ponder as the next point of light illuminates an essential quality of how we might understand the Other to engage in meaningful relationships.

I-THOU RELATIONSHIP

Mayes refers to the 20th-century theologian Martin Buber who speaks of *I-Thou* relationships between oneself and the Other, which can occur between two people, between consciousness and the unconscious, or even between oneself and one's experience with the sacred. What is essential is the notion of being joined with another in mutual interdependence. Buber writes, "I become through my relation to the *Thou*; as I become *I*, I say *Thou*. All real living is meeting" (Buber, 1937, p. 11). In other words, each encounter with another can be seen as an encounter with ourselves, and vice versa, so that separation of self and other can begin to dissolve.

The abiding commonality in I-Thou relationships is that the presence of the Other is honored and listened to. And while there will inevitably be differences between us, there is not necessarily a hierarchy of value—both sides being integral to any true relationship. In the realm of the psyche, Jung says, "The ego takes the lead, but the unconscious must be allowed to have its say too—*audiatur et altera pars* (Jung, 1969a, p. 88). Translated from the Latin, this phrase means "may the other side also be heard."

I believe Jung drew this reference from *The Eumenides*, a play written by Aeschylus in 485 B.C., in which Athena, the goddess of justice, speaking at the trial of Orestes, convinces the creatures of darkness, the Furies, to listen to another side of an argument. Initially, the Furies wanted to prosecute Orestes for his crimes, but after listening to Athena describe the long line of murder and retaliation within Orestes's family, they changed their minds and voted to acquit him.

In this tale of murder and retaliation, Athena won the Furies over with the promise of success and a seat upon the golden throne in the underworld. She said to them, "Go then. Sped by majestic sacrifice from these, plunge beneath the ground . . . success in the end" (Aeschylus, 1959, lines 1006–1013). To "plunge beneath the ground" could be likened to a descent into the unconscious where the Furies must encounter their own shadow, and no matter what they find there, they were welcomed to sit on a "golden throne" by Athena. This could mean that by facing into our own darkness, golden compassion will rise within us. Our ability to look within and to "relate to the feelings of otherness within ourselves" (Romanyshyn, 2013a, p. 340) is what's needed to develop the genuine kindness of I-Thou relationships and thus to be able to share it with others in the world.

DEATH

The final point of light that I will attend to from *Teaching Mysteries* is the value of remembering death, not as something "macabre" as Mayes says, but rather, as something that is "life-giving." Mayes says that "it is only in fully embracing the fact that one will die that one can begin to live" (2005, p. 73). Endings are inevitable and reveal the ultimate need to practice the art of closure and of good-byes. A classroom enlivened with an awareness of endings can support profound realizations throughout the day and act as a reminder of the ephemeral nature of the moments we share.

But it is classrooms enlivened with all of Mayes's points of light that bode well for the future, for they connect us to the essence of who we are; they open our hearts to each other, and they reveal the message that the world is alive, life is valuable, and we belong.

ROBERT ROMANYSHYN'S METHOD

I will focus next on the application of Romanyshyn's method, which I believe can make Mayes points of light even more accessible. Romanyshyn draws from Jung's concept of active imagination (e.g., 1966, 1969a, Jung, 1971), where dialogue with the other reveals what lay hidden in the depths of the psyche.

Step One: Setting the Stage

This first step is akin to the creation of a *temenos*, the building of a sacred precinct in an atmosphere of welcome. This begins by softening around the edges of the conscious mind, where one is "freed of literal and factual density . . . [and which] requires a hermeneutics of understanding rather than an empirics of explanation" (Romanyshyn, 2013a, p. 87).

The word *hermeneutics* is associated with the Greek god Hermes, who was thought to have been able to move between the world of mortals and the world of the divine, which is seen as emblematic of the interpretive act of translating meaning from one plane of existence into that of another (Kerenyi, 1980, p. 163). The hermeneutics of understanding is therefore apropos to this step as it occupies what Romanyshyn calls *a ritual space of reverie*, a "middle space between waking and dreaming . . . the gap between the language of the day and that of the night . . . between conscious understanding and unconscious depth" (Romanyshyn, 2013a, p. 87).

This is the realm of the imaginal, as written about by the late Persian scholar Henry Corbin (1969), and it is thought to exist between the visible, external, sensory realm of material bodies and the realm of pure spirit, soul, or the divine. It can feel here as if one is in a waking dream, where thoughts, feelings, and images rise and fall beyond control of the conscious mind. There is a sense of boundarylessness, an infinite egress between wakefulness and sleep, between thinking and imagining, being and not being, in which we come face to face with the spaciousness of the unknown.

As unsettling as this open-ended experience can be, however, it is within this realm that new forms and ideas can be born. They manifest as fantasy images and "are the bridge that spans the gap between the unconscious depths and [our] conscious understandings of it" (Romanyshyn, 2013a, p. 141). Jung speaks of fantasy images as carrying a life force, not unlike pregnancy itself. Jung says that the German word *betrachten* "means to make pregnant. . . . And if it is pregnant, then something is due to come out of it; it is alive, it produces, it multiplies" (Jung 1930–1934a, Vol. 6, Lecture 1, May 4, 1932, p. 3). Fantasies are the children of the imaginal realm who invite us to exist in the complexity of their imagery.

The ritual space of reverie creates a container for what's to come and encourages the willing acceptance of whatever will be will be. Romanyshyn says, "Reverie is something one falls into. Reverie happens to us. One can set the stage for its appearance, but one does not direct the action" (Romanyshyn, 2013a, p. 142). The ego mind is given a place to rest and to play in an ambiance of trust so that it might relax into the unknown and discover something new.

Step Two: Invitations

The second step that can support the emergence of Mayes's points of light in the classroom is to extend invitations to fantasy figures at four different levels: the personal, where feelings, thoughts and memories are conversed with; the cultural, which includes different historical periods, races, genders, and socioeconomic backgrounds; the collective and the archetypal, which represents common psychic patterns, such as Trickster, Lover, Adversary, and Sage; and the ecological level, which includes "those other beings who share the space of creation with us" (Romanyshyn, 2013b, p. 323).

The overarching quality of these invitations and their resulting dialogues is that the figures be engaged with in a playful way. Jung said, "The dynamic principle of fantasy is play. . . . Without this playing with fantasy no creative work has ever yet come to birth. The debt we owe to the play of imagination is incalculable" (Jung, 1971, p. 63). To play means to be open, to suspend disbelief, and to welcome fantasy figures as companions in a game of mutual discovery.

It could be considered *mutual* because it may be that these fantasy figures inhabit the world objectively and beyond the limitations of our perceptions. While such figures are traditionally thought to be merely symbolic, Romanyshyn suggests that we might still "be open to [their] possible autonomous reality" (Romanyshyn, 2013b, p. 232). This is important to consider as it can indicate that we live in an enchanted universe touched by the presence of Others.

Step Three: Waiting with Hospitality

When ambiance has been created and the invitations sent out, the third step Romanyshyn speaks of is to wait with hospitality. This may be the most difficult step, however, as it necessitates that we be patient in an uncertain world. But this struggle might be exactly what is needed for the conscious mind to loosen its grip so that images and symbols from the unconscious can emerge and provide a deeper sense of meaning. Waiting with hospitality is to "wait without expectation or desire for a response and to quiet the internal critic who tells us that we are wasting time, or doing it wrong, or [that] the process is foolish" (Romanyshyn, 2013b, p. 323). We can learn to tolerate and even welcome feelings of doubt and confusion as necessary emotions on our journey with destiny woven together by the Fates.

Step Four: Engaging the Others in the Work

After the first three steps have been attended to adequately, a conversation with the Other can begin—which brings us to step four. There are two parts to this step: the first is to give the Other a form of some sort, and the second is to reflect upon it. This can be done through writing, drawing, painting, sculpting, or embodying the figures in movement. But what is most essential is that we accept and acknowledge whatever it is that wants to come through. That is, we intuitively trust the expression of the deeper psyche, honor it as a Thou and treat it hospitably with patience, kindness, and optimism for what might emerge.

And then, once the figures are tangible and available to be conversed with, the task is to engage with them until a sense of completion can be reached. Romanyshyn says, "The key here is to remember that presence precedes meaning" (Romanyshyn, 2013b, p. 323), wherein, we let the images range around and arrive in their fullness before making judgments about them.

The forms that emerge out of our experiences may be familiar and comfortable, or they may reveal things that we would rather not know about ourselves, those things that Jung calls the *shadow* (e.g., Jung, 1970). To engage the Other in the work is to accept the shadow and everything that arrives with it, the good, the bad, the beautiful, and the ugly—with equanimity, and only then, to attempt to make sense of it. It is a dance between experience and perception on the one hand, and expression and meaning on the other. Jung says, "The ideal case would be if these two aspects could exist side by side or rhythmically succeed each other: that is, if there were an alternation of creation and understanding" (Jung, 1969a, p. 86). The process of growth is to witness, create, converse, and reflect.

Jungian psychologist Marie-Louise von Franz (1980) has conceptualized it in this way: empty the "mad mind" of the ego, let unconscious fantasy images arise, give them some form of expression, ethically engage with them, and then, apply them to ordinary life. This process supports the Mayesian psycho-spiritual concepts of creating sacred space, thinking symbolically, cultivating I-Thou relationships, and following one's destiny.

As a teacher, I welcome Mayes ideas into the classroom with my students so that we might feel the support and guidance from a deeper source and come to trust our own experiences so that reciprocal relationships between self and other may be fostered, where what we give and what we gain become two sides of the same coin. Mayes gives us concepts to hold onto while the reality of the invisible world makes its way to our consciousness and leads us into a place of communion with something greater. Transcendence is our birthright, but we have to cultivate it, or we will become victims of the negative ideological "certainties" of those who think they have something to sell.

Mayes's points of light in *Teaching Mysteries* are like the *scintillae*, the sparks of light that Jung speaks about that compound into the *lumen naturae.* Jung says, "[T]he light of nature, the *lumen naturae*, is a light with a fiery longing to enkindle" (CW8, p. 194). And Mayes's profound opus does just this.

REFERENCES

Aeschylus. (1959). The Eumenides (R. Lattimore, Trans.). In D. Grene & R. Lattimore (Eds.), *The Complete Greek Tragedies. Vol. 1.* (pp. 133–71). The University of Chicago Press.

Bekiempis, V. (2021, December 4). Michigan shooting: suspect's parents held on $1m bond after capture. *The Guardian: U.S. Edition.* https://www.theguardian.com/us-news/2021/dec/04/michigan-shooting-suspects-parents-held-on-1m-bond-james-jennifer-crumbley

Buber, M. (1937). *I and thou* (R. G. Smith, Trans.). T. & T. Clark.

Corbin. H. (1969). *Alone with the alone: Creative imagination in the Sufism of Ibn 'Arabī.* Princeton University Press.

Jung, C. G. (1933). *Visions: Notes of the Seminar Given in 1930–1940, Vol. II* (February 1, 1933).

Jung, C. G. (1930–1934a). *Interpretations of Visions,* privately mimeographed seminar notes of Mary Foote, 1941.

Jung, C. G. (1961). *Memories, dreams, reflections.* Random House.

Jung, C. G. (1966). On the relation of analytical psychology to poetry (R. F. C. Hull, Trans.). In H. Read et al. (Eds.), *The collected works of C. G. Jung: Vol.15. Spirit in man, art, and literature* (pp. 65–83). Princeton University Press. (Original work published 1922)

Jung, C. G. (1968). Individual dream symbolism in relation to alchemy (R. F. C. Hull, Trans.). In H. Read et al. (Eds.), *The collected works of C. G. Jung: Vol. 12. Psychology and alchemy* (2nd ed., pp. 38–223). Princeton University Press. (Original work published 1936)

Jung, C. G. (1969a). The transcendent function (R. F. C. Hull, Trans.). In H. Read et al. (Eds.), *The collected works of C. G. Jung: Vol. 8. Structure and dynamics of the psyche* (2nd ed., pp. 67–91). Princeton University Press. (Original work published 1958)

Jung, C. G. (1969b). The structure of the psyche (R. F. C. Hull, Trans.). In H. Read et al. (Eds.), *The collected works of C. G. Jung: Vol. 8. Structure and dynamics of the psyche* (2nd ed., pp. 139–58). Princeton University Press. (Original work published 1931)

Jung, C. G. (1969c). Synchronicity: An acausal connecting principle (R. F. C. Hull, Trans.). In H. Read et al. (Eds.), *The collected works of C. G. Jung: Vol. 8. Structure and dynamics of the psyche* (2nd ed., pp. 417–519). Princeton University Press. (Original work published 1952)

Jung, C. G. (1970). A psychological view of conscience. (R. F. C. Hull, Trans.). In H. Head et al. (Eds.), *The collected works of C. G. Jung: Vol. 10. Civilization in transition* (2nd ed., pp. 437–55). Princeton University Press. (Original work published 1958).

Jung. C. G. (1971). *The collected works of C. G. Jung: Vol. 6. Psychological Types.* (R. F. C. Hull, Trans.). In H. Read et al. (Eds.), Princeton University Press. (Original work published 1921)

Jung, C. G. (1976). The symbolic life (R. F. C. Hull, Trans.). In H. Read et al. (Eds.), *The collected works of C. G. Jung: Vol.18. The symbolic life* (pp. 267–90). Princeton University Press. (Original work published 1954)

Jung, C. G. (1977). Does the world stand on the verge of spiritual rebirth? In *Jung Speaking* (pp. 67–75). Princeton University Press.

Kerenyi, K. (1980). *The gods of the Greeks*. Thames and Hudson.

Mayes, C. (2016). *An introduction to the collected works of C. G. Jung: Spirit as psyche.* Rowman & Littlefield.

Mayes, C. (2005). *Teaching Mysteries: Foundations of spiritual pedagogy*. University Press of America, Inc.

Romanyshyn, R. D. (2013a). *The wounded researcher: Research with soul in mind.* Spring Journal, Inc.

Romanyshyn, R. D. (2013b). Making a place for unconscious factors in research. *International Journal of Multiple Research Approaches*, 7(3), 314–29.

Von Franz, M. L. (1980). *Alchemy: An introduction to the symbolism and the psychology.* Inner City Books.

Chapter 4

Soul-Care

Tending the Flame of the Numinous in Children's Education

Cynthia Schumacher

Expelled from American public-school classrooms are the souls of children. In the context of this exploration, the soul is defined as a child's inner capacity for knowing and learning through the psychic processes of imagination, intuition, the body, and emotions. These are vital *educative* processes—the ground from which children develop a sense of personal identity, meaning, and the inner resiliency of faith.

This chapter examines different points of view to answer the following questions: "Why regard American education as soulless? How can public schools invite the soul back into the classroom? What are the obstacles to such a project?" In answering these questions, I present two depth psychological considerations for the soul-care of children in American education.

First, we must nurture and preserve children's intrinsic capacity for *numinous* or transpersonal experience so that they may bring forth that which is within them—an innate relationship to their souls. Here, I examine potential doorways to the inner sanctum of the *numinosum* of the soul and the barriers erected—including Western modernity—to soulful experiences in American classrooms.

Second, through the principles of depth psychology, teachers can lead as models of spiritual commitment that exemplify a foundation for children to discover and engage transpersonal ways of learning and knowing. These soulful educative processes foster the psychospiritual development of the whole child—both the ego as the personal self and the soul as the transpersonal self.

Further, I anticipate and address arguments against soul-care in public school education that many deem "spiritual" or "religious" education. Some deem *any* form of such education as a breach of the Establishment Clause of the First Amendment, prohibiting the sanctioning of a particular religion, or indeed religion in general, in public institutions. Despite these arguments against bringing so-called "spiritual" or "religious" terms and ideas to children's education, there is growing momentum for transformative change in American public-school education.

A SACRED DUTY: SOUL-CARE OF CHILDREN IN AMERICAN EDUCATION

Jung (1969c) states that the religious function of the human psyche is the ground from which *all* psychic processes occur. According to Jung (1969b), the totality of the psyche contains the ego-consciousness and the unconscious. The unconscious includes the personal subconscious and the collective unconscious. The personal subconscious includes forgotten and repressed material of the individual, most of which was at one point conscious but was banished to the subconscious because it is too painful to bear.

On the other hand, the collective unconscious is the archetypal or transpersonal realm of the psyche—the ancestral heritage common to all humans (Jung, 1969a). Although the collective unconscious exercises a determining effect on consciousness, the individual is not directly aware of it, owing to its ancient primal roots, on one hand, and its transcendental potential, on the other hand. Jung (1954) defines "integration of consciousness" as the development of the ego-consciousness from the matrix of the unconscious (p. 52).

The whole picture boils down to a tri-stratal model, as Clifford Mayes (2020) has recently argued, drawing on psychoanalytic terminology. Thus, the origin of all forms of the conscious, subconscious, and conscious mind is the collective unconscious, which we may therefore call the *primary process*. The subconscious—"wedged," as it were, between the conscious mind and the collective unconscious—is the *secondary* process. Finally, the conscious mind, as a product of both the personal subconscious and collective unconscious, is thus the *tertiary* process. Parents are crucial in the early emergence and establishment of ego-consciousness in their children's lives; then teachers provide the "means of strengthening in a purposeful way" this dynamic (Jung, 1954, p. 52).

The soul-care of a child is a sacred duty for all those who participate in the child's life. So much can go wrong when, in the beginning, so much is already right. In other words, when a child is born, his/her soul is yet unfettered by the weight of deficient childcare—soul-care. Let's face it, the *perfect* parent, caregiver, or educator does not exist. However, in the soul-care of a child, parents, caregivers, and educators have a sacred obligation to provide as mindful an approach in the support and guidance of a child's ego *and* soul (i.e., psychospiritual) development as they possibly can.

As Winnicott (1992) famously put it: No parent can be perfect, nor, indeed, should they be. Perfectionism is a neurotic position, even a schizoid one in Melanie Klein's (1975/1932) terms. Rather, what the parent both can and should be is "good enough." This means that the parent has done his or her best, rests content in that knowledge, and that the child finds itself in that realistic care.

As a mindful approach to aiding a child's ego development and tending the flame of their soul, I suggest that a path to the soul be left open, unencumbered by adult doctrinal religious expectations and negative biases to unique transpersonal experiences. In so doing, a child can recognize and find meaning in personal numinous experiences, establishing a faith beyond any religious institution or in concert with it. According to Lionel Corbett (2012), in *Psyche and the Sacred: Spirituality Beyond the Sacred*, this faith, based on a child's intimate, meaningful encounters with a transcendent *otherness*, manifests from the transpersonal or archetypal level of the collective unconscious and not the "doctrine, dogma, or sacred texts" of organized religion (p. 14).

IMAGES OF SOULLESSNESS IN
AMERICAN EDUCATION

Greg Nixon (1997) addresses the meaninglessness—soullessness—of American education:

> Because, no matter how sugar-coated the pill has become—no matter how many research projects have been undertaken to make it more palatable—schooling still asks people to give up the potential of their individual souls for the sake of "the greater good" of the collective. (p. 57)

I suggest that this point of view of American schools evokes the image of the Borg, an alien group featured in the television series *Star Trek: The Next Generation* (1987–1994) and the film *Star Trek: First Contact* (1996). The Borg ship houses the implants of captive humans (and extraterrestrials) stripped of their humanity—their souls—and assimilated as cybernetic slave drones to a hive mind of the "Collective," whose mantra is "Resistance is futile. You will be assimilated."

According to Nixon (1997), when the *collective* of the school system works, then the student *assimilates* into the dominant social order, permitting the "desires and fears" of the collective to infiltrate her psyche (p. 56). I suggest that, like the Borg, students participate in what Nixon (1997) asserts is "a subtle life-term form of self-sacrifice, the person becomes a citizen whose moods reflect the rise and fall of the GDP [Gross Domestic Product]" (Nixon, 1997, p. 56). Both desire and fear feed the machine of educational policymaking that gave rise to standardized education and the dominance of STEM (i.e., science, technology, engineering, mathematics) curricula, which serve first and foremost the nation's economic growth. Desire launches young people into the hive mind of ever-devouring consumers, chasing the cultural ideal of success limited to monetary and material gains. For assimilated children schooled in fear of failure, the ideal becomes a haunting mirage that only a few achieve.

The image of the American education system as the mechanized assimilation of children and, I would add, their dedicated teachers into the "Collective" as soulless "Borg drones" is a striking image of horror. Alan A. Block (1997), in *I'm Only Bleeding: Education as the Practice of Violence Against Children*, states that the American public school's assimilation of children is an act of violence. The violence of assimilation takes place because children threaten "the project of modernity" that values "achievement, order, control, and hierarchy" (p. 10).

Standardized education and STEM curricula are the instruments of assimilation and violence that enslaves children and shackles teachers to the collective social order. The real threat to the project of modernity is the souls of children and imaginative, playful, and embodied ways of learning—soulful ways of learning—that are psychologically and spiritually nourishing but not necessarily economically profitable for the nation. The requirement that children leave their souls outside the classroom is the violence of assimilation.

However, if we dare to examine the education system as the assimilation of children into the collective of the American cultural imperative of consumerism and materialism, then perhaps this image will provide insight and ideas for transformation and offer an invitation for children's souls to enter the classroom. What I am seeking are soulful ways of learning that nourish and preserve each child's intrinsic capacity for numinous experiences that engender the soul's homecoming into the fullness of being as each child grows into adulthood.

The Flame of the Numinous and the Flame Retardant—Western Modernity

Rudolf Otto (1958) defines *numinous* experience as invoking a "*mysterium tremendum*" with the feeling states of awe and fascination (p. 12). What early childhood teacher has not walked into a classroom with a new puppy, bunny, or some other of nature's creatures and heard a collective "ahh" from the children, seen the light of delight in their eyes, and the softening expressions of joy on their faces. Numinous states such as these involve contact with nature—*all creatures great and small.* So too, the ever-changing shapes of white clouds and birds in flight against a canvas of blue sky or the sound of the wind singing through the trees that take one beyond ordinary reality into a transpersonal state of consciousness. Transpersonal consciousness conveys the soul more fully into one's being as a state of wholeness—a state of grace. Tragically, within the system of American standardized education, children are given meager opportunities for soulful states of grace.

One obstacle to American public schools offering occasions for these soulful states is that "we can't get there from here." The "here" of Western modernity, reflected in American education, suffers from a split that creates polarized binaries in ways of knowing and learning—the rational and irrational, the *abstract* mind and the *numinous* body, objective scientific consciousness and subjective imaginal unconscious. Entrenched cultural views about what American education should be valorize rational, objective consciousness of mind over the soul's subjective, transrational consciousness. The flame of a child's soul diminishes when opportunities for soulful ways of learning—imagination, intuition, body, nature, play, and creativity—are inadequate or absent in the classroom.

POTENTIAL DOORWAYS INTO THE
NUMINOUS IN AMERICAN EDUCATION

Young children easily enter and experience numinous states of consciousness in contact with nature. Corbett (2012) writes that children are highly sensitive to the numinous if that sensitivity is not "blunted by exposure to social expectations" or by emulating adult attitudes (p. 27). According to Corbett (2012), "any activity that is a source of passionate concern in the child's life may be numinous" (p. 27). These sources of passionate concern are the doorways by which children enter fields of enchantment through embodied contact with nature and other soulful ways of knowing and learning.

As a child, I remember one magical experience of *passionate concern* while playing with friends. We were gathering bits of broken glass—remarkably many colors—from an undisturbed treelined rural roadside, thickly layered with leaves, pine needles, and rocks; soon after, we washed the pieces, until they sparkled like diamonds, emeralds, rubies, and sapphires. This treasure hunt felt magical and outside of time.

One-year later, my friends and I tried to play the same game again, but I did not experience the same sense of enchantment—numinosity. Deeply disappointed, I vividly recall in my child's mind thinking, "Why do I not feel the same way?" There was a palpable sense of loss as I dearly wanted to conjure the magic from the previous year. In the passing of time, my child-self somehow lost the capacity for the transpersonal experience in the magical enchantment of play in nature so keenly felt just one year prior.

Jerome Bernstein's *Living in the Borderland: The Evolution of Consciousness and the Challenge of Healing Trauma* (2005) describes a child's transpersonal experience of "Borderland" consciousness as "'sacred' . . . beyond rational experience, and which carries a feeling of numinosity" (p. 11). Bernstein (2005) asserts that "unless they are shamed or cognitively yanked out of it," children under the age of six or seven naturally experience the numinosity of Borderland consciousness rooted in the collective unconscious (p. 87).

Here, Western modernity's bias and fear of the invisible "irrational" unconscious restricts soulful ways of knowing applied to educational curricula. The *otherness* of the invisible "borderlands" is a threat to modernity's hierarchy of control and containment that serves the objectives of the nation *for the nation* and not the children serving time in public school institutions.

BARRIERS TO THE NUMINOUS IN EDUCATION

Unfortunately, during the school year, the frantic race to achieve high marks on standardized tests leaves little time or curricular space for children's natural inclination for numinous experiences. In the push to fill minds with facts and figures, American public schools neglect and even obstruct children's psychospiritual development, stripping children of their natural sensitivity to the *numinous* in the race to build a viable workforce for the country's economic growth; children's souls are expelled from the classroom stifling their capacity to experience the *numinous*.

This economic race is undoubtedly why Lawrence Cremin, the greatest of all U.S. educational historians, warned in his concluding work, *American Education: The Metropolitan Experience* (1988), that the trend of U.S. public education in the 20th century had been toward the increasing corporatization of schooling in the service of emerging global capitalism. Cremin's claim would be backed by the newly emerging disciplines of psychology and sociology. These would not only provide "scientific evidence" of the need for the bureaucratization of education; they would also show how to do it.

Picking up where President Eisenhower left off in his final address to the nation in 1961, in which the chief executive warned of the growth of the "military-industrial complex" as the prime threat to democracy in the 20th century, Cremin (1988) now amplified on the theme, warning that the paramount threat to democracy in the 21st century would be the apocalyptic emergence of a military-industrial-*educational* complex. It would train students, for no other purpose than, to be obedient "worker citizens" (Spring, 1976) in the functioning of the new Total State. Education would now not exist, as John Dewey (1916) had dreamed it would, in the service of democracy, nor, as Boyd Bode (1921) had hoped it would, in the service of canonical knowledge garnered in the 2,000 years of Western history. No. Education would now become the prime tool in establishing and maintaining the military and industrial supremacy of the United States geopolitically.

This was the stated goal of the *Nation at Risk* report of 1986 and the goal that has informed virtually every major policy statement on education issued from the presidential level since that time (Watras, 2002). This could not be more antithetical to the higher purposes for education for which I am arguing. Certainly, schooling must serve practical economic and technological purposes. But when this is its primary orientation and *raison d'etre*, then the transmission of the principles and practices of American democracy, and indeed any awareness of the entire Western philosophical and artistic tradition, are in peril of being quite forgotten in the hearts and minds of our children. This bodes ill for our future, individually and collectively.

IN DEFENSE OF THE NUMINOUS AS
THE HEART OF EDUCATION

The light of the *numinous* is the soul light, a flame that burns in the heart of every human—adult and children alike. Following Meister Eckhart, Jung calls the soul "the *image of God*" (1971, p. 250). Further, Jung (1977) defines the self as the *imago Dei*—God-images—symbols manifesting from the archetypal realm of the collective unconscious in all their multivalency. Like a pilot light in the kitchen stove, the soul light images require attention, awaiting the spark that, as an adult, ignites the fire in the process of self-education.

Jung defines *self-education* (i.e., individuation, self-realization, soul-realization) as an indirect learning method that allows adults to educate themselves regarding their unique psychic development (1954, p. 58). Through self-education, the individual strives to embody the unconscious soul more fully into the personality's conscious psychic totality. Jung states that individuation is "the recognition of our wholeness or completeness as a binding personal commitment" (1969c, p. 727).

However, according to Jung, "at present we educate people only up to the point where they can earn a living and marry; then education ceases altogether, as though a complete mental outfit had been acquired" (1954, p. 57). Jung (1954) asserts that the process of individuation should continue throughout the person's life. However, the great majority of people do not do so, primarily because of the extreme moral and emotional difficulty of looking at one's own shadow. Wrote Jung,

> The shadow is a moral problem that challenges the whole ego-personality, for no one can become conscious of the shadow without considerable moral effort. To become conscious of it involves recognizing the dark aspects of the personality as present and real. This act is the essential condition for any kind of self-knowledge" (1969c, p. 8)

Jung (1954) admonishes that the methods of individuation do not apply to children, and the focus for children's education needs to be the development of a healthy ego. However, I suggest that as adults, we could more easily recognize self-images—soul images—during the individuating process as adults if offered a more psychospiritually supportive education as children. This type of education would allow children to derive meaning and, thus knowledge, from the images manifesting from the archetypal or transpersonal realm.

Rejecting Jung's injunction that individuation applies only to adults, in *Children as Individuals*, Michael Fordham (1994) contends that the individuation processes apply to children as well. Transpersonal consciousness houses the flame of our souls from infancy through childhood and into adulthood. The door to the inner sanctum of these psychic processes left open for the transpersonal or the soul allows children to retain their natural capacity for numinous experience, profound creativity, and self-discovery.

The archetypal or religious function of the psyche by which the individual experiences the numinous occur indirectly through consciousness or happens spontaneously—bubbling up from the unconscious (Jung, 1969a). Either way, recognizing and valuing these inner experiences from the vast expanse of a transpersonal reality are rich educational opportunities that allow children grown to adulthood to come home to their souls in the process of individuation.

ADVOCATES FOR SOUL CARE IN AMERICAN EDUCATION

Many learned individuals advocate for the provision and care for the psychospiritual health of children in education. In developing archetypal pedagogy, Clifford Mayes (2004, 2005, 2007, 2010, 2016a, 2016b, 2017, 2020) makes an invaluable contribution, providing a Jungian and post-Jungian perspective and approach to transformative education. Mayes's (2007, 2010, 2017) archetypal pedagogy seeks to facilitate the psychodynamic and psychospiritual development of both teachers and students.

In *Archetype, Culture, and the Individual in Education: The Three Pedagogical Narratives*, Mayes asserts that standardized education forces students into mundane memorization of facts and figures that *do not* interest the students because the facts do not cohere into any intellectually clear or emotionally compelling structures. This is an "emotional subjugation [assimilation to the collective] and a cognitive self-mutilation [violence]" (Mayes, 2020, p. 114). Mayes insists that the educative curriculum must create dynamic interest for each student—a resonance to their inner subjectivity—asserting that this inner "subjectivity is the spiritual 'engineering' that launches cognition on its every mission" (2020, p. 112). This "spiritual 'engineering'" is the soul as the seat of our subjective experience of feeling-states, bodily senses, intuition, and imagination. When we shut the door to these inner psychic processes—what Jung refers to as the "religious function" of the soul—leaving the soul outside the classroom, opportunities for soulful ways of knowing and learning are lost (1970, p. 12).

Other advocates for soul care in education include Marissa Crawford and Graham Rossiter in *Reasons for Living: Education and Young People's Search for Meaning, Identity, and Spirituality*. Crawford and Rossiter advocate attending to meaning, identity, and spirituality in order to fully support adolescent students in today's culture (2006, p. xxii). All three constructs are vitally interwoven threads onto which depth psychological perspectives, and archetypal pedagogy in particular, have cast considerable light.

In *The Spirit of the Child*, David Hay with Rebecca Nye (2006) argue for the return of the soul to the classroom, making a case for spirituality in education as an essential ingredient for the psychospiritual development of children. Also, in *To Know as We Are Known: Education as a Spiritual Journey*, Parker Palmer states that in education, "we must recover from our spiritual traditions the models and methods of knowing as an act of love" (1993, p. 9). Acts of love are acts of "passionate concern" that evoke compassion, relationship, ethics, and moral understanding—hallmarks of an education rooted in psychospiritual pedagogy.

DEBATES AND OTHER PROBLEMATIC DELIBERATIONS

Any proposal for American public schools to attend to a child's psychospiritual development is seen by many as contrary to the First Amendment's statement that Congress shall make no law either establishing or promoting religion—the so-called "Establishment Clause." The matter is far from simple, however, and has led to various U.S. Supreme Court decisions and dicta regarding religion in the public schools.

Conflicting messages on the interaction between public and private education ultimately led to *Lemon v. Kurtzman* (1971), which established a test to determine whether a school was engaging in the establishment of religion on campus and in the curriculum. The resulting three-part Lemon test required that a curriculum (1) have a secular purpose, (2) has a principal or primary effect that neither advances *nor inhibits* religion, and (3) must not foster an excessive entanglement of a school with religion.

More recently, *Agostini et al. v. Felton et al.* (1997), seems to have replaced the Lemon test. Like its predecessor, it has a three-part test of constitutionality. To be constitutional, a curriculum cannot (1) result in government indoctrination, (2) define students by reference to religion, or (3) create an excessive government entanglement with a church or churches. This less stringent test may have opened the door for greater interaction between the church and state. Recent cases involving limited open forums, religiously sponsored clubs, and prayer at school functions continue the debate. Based on the *Good News Club v. Milford Central School* (2001) case, it now appears nearly impossible to reach the constitutional threshold for religious establishment.

In general, it seems that teachers and administrators tend intuitively to approach the topic of religion in the classroom along the lines suggested in the famous Supreme Court decision *Abington Township, Pennsylvania, et al. v. Schempp et al.* (1963).

Here, Justice Goldberg, writing the majority opinion, said that religious matters *can* be introduced in schools if they (1) are relevant to the issues under analysis in the curriculum, (2) are age appropriate to the students, and (3) are presented even-handedly by the teacher with no indication that she favors one religious viewpoint over another or that she favors a non-religious viewpoint.

Nevertheless, despite the ambiguity of the situation and the general principle in *Abington*, many teachers and principals still do find it to be unacceptable to have any mention whatsoever of God in children's education because of ill-informed parental outrage if they do. This is especially true of parents who are atheists, agnostics, or members of marginalized religion whose beliefs are rarely even mentioned in any forms of public discourse.

Greg Nixon (1997), in asking "What god does educational experience serve?," points to an alarming contradiction. Although the Constitution mandates the separation of church and state, state-mandated education *serves the state*, and herein lies a problem. During the inception of this nation, to counter idleness and the "Devil," our Puritan cultural heritage evoked the god of work, materialism, and success (Nixon, 1997). With this early beginning, the trajectory of American education serving the nation's economic growth became the supreme god (Nixon, 1997).

The cultural attitude of the American education system aligns with Western modernity's biases and fears of the unconscious as a threat to the hegemony of corporately determined policymaking in education. Thus, soulful ways of learning threaten the nation's agenda to produce a workforce and grow the economy, and so, state-mandated education barred children's souls from the classroom.

Furthermore, in the race to generate a productive workforce for the country, the public school system blinds children's eyes to see, deafens their ears to hear, and closes their hearts to feel the presence of the *numinosum* of their souls. Wexler describes the dichotomy between two types of schooling: An education that fosters "the integration of body-mind-energy [soul], a social metaphysic of expansive presence in the here and now, is the antithetical curriculum to the performance-based petrification and containment of the soul in corporatist, Toyota-production style schooling" (2008, p. 12).

How can we endeavor to discuss what might be gained by an education that attends more closely to the flame of a child's soul, nurturing and preserving a child's potential for numinous experience? In terms of a child's schooling, perhaps the lexicon used—words like religious, spiritual, and God—with the associated diversity in meanings and values, hobbles the discussion of soul-care in education before it begins. Nevertheless, using a more neutral vocabulary may cause less conflict and garner more support for implementing change for supporting personal faith through soul-care in education. Corbett suggests considering religious experience in terms of an archetypal experience and "individual connection to the divine," advocating for the etymological origins of "the word 'religious' by using it in a specific technical sense" and not implying "adherence to a particular creed" (1996, p. 63).

The etymology of "religion" comes from "*religare*," which means to reconnect two things that had once been joined but came to mean specifically the reconnection of the human and divine spheres (Etymology Online Dictionary, n.d.). Now, if we take religion to convey the idea of the bond between a child and her soul; and if we further assume that imagination and other pathways of knowing come from the inner sanctum of the soul, then perhaps we can manage to create a less contentious means of talking about "religious" education.

Indeed, Mayes discusses the role of the teacher who facilitates this bond between "the student's biographical narrative with the Divinity that invests a classroom with matters of spiritual import" (2020, p. 115). This link occurs "anywhere the acts of learning meld the individual and the eternal in the saving fires of education *impassioned*" (Mayes, 2020, p. 115).

For these subjective experiences, the word numinous becomes less threatening when we use it to denote children's delight in nature, the enchantment of play, the joy of painting, performing music, sculpting with clay, or building a model plane. We can speak of how these experiences foster inner faith, resiliency, self-discovery, and psychological well-being. We can also discuss giving children more time for deep immersion into the archetypal waters of imagination, creativity, and nature, leading to happier and more fulfilled adults and society. Regrettably, today's educational system offers few opportunities for archetypal, religious, or numinous experiences by any other name.

WHERE ARE WE LEADING CHILDREN?

From the time I was in kindergarten to the time I raised three children to the present, as I witness the education of five grandchildren, American public-school education has morphed into an institution wholly immersed in the mindset of pounding the standardized curriculum into the minds of children. This mindset raises the question: "What does it mean to educate?" Although an enormously broad topic, here I use the lens of archetypal pedagogy to examine two phrases derived from the etymological root of the word *educate, educere,* which means to "bring out" and "lead forth" (Etymology Online Dictionary, n.d.). The questions then arise with children's education: "Where are we *leading* children, and what are we *bringing out*?"

In leading children, from what place do they begin? Jung (1954) describes the beginning stages of childhood as living in a state of what French anthropologist Lévy-Bruhl attributed to primal people and termed *participation mystique. Participation mystique* is an undifferentiated state of consciousness in which self-identity or ego-consciousness has yet to be established, evoking a lived experience of the numinous (Jung, 1954). Here, then, a Jungian perspective of a child's education beginning at birth indicates we lead a child out of the miasma of the first developmental stage of undifferentiated consciousness. In other words, we nurture and guide a child from no sense of identity, ego, or the self to the establishment of a self-identity—ego-consciousness. Formal schooling assists the child in this development.

According to Jung (1954), "methodical teaching of the curriculum . . . is at most half of the meaning of school. The other half is the real psychological education made possible through the personality of the teacher. This education means guiding the child into the larger world" (Jung, 1954, p. 56). Indeed, a teacher guides a child in her relationship with the outer objective world. For this relationship to be healthy, a child needs to establish ego-structures that facilitate her ability to develop boundaries, make decisions, and assist her when encountering the vicissitudes of the larger world of life.

However, the quality of this relationship with the outer objective world is predicated on a child's connection to the inner subjective world. By attending to a child's inner relationship through soulful educative processes, the teacher becomes a *psychopomp*—a term meaning a guide for the soul into the under-world (Mayes, 2017). As a soul guide, the teacher influences the student by modeling the path of individuation by attending to her inner soul light. Jung states that this modeling is of greater import than "merely pounding the curriculum into the child" (1954, p. 55).

By modeling the path of individuation, the teacher is a model of faith as well. The etymological roots and meaning of "faith" include trust, confidence, belief, reliance, and loyalty (Etymology Online Dictionary, n.d.). What if we taught children to direct their faith inward to their souls so that they could discover and nurture trust and confidence within their being? For a child, this faith engenders a sense of believing in oneself, self-reliance, and a loyalty to Polonius's stated ideal in *Hamlet*: "To thine own self be true." Therefore, in transformative education, the teacher attends to the educative processes that develop the student's relationship with the outer world *and* a faith relationship with the inner world, fostering the development of the whole child—both the ego (i.e., personal self) and the soul (i.e., transpersonal self).

The development of the whole child is not a priority in standardized education. The concretization of standardized curricula appears to leave little flexibility for transformative education processes. Nevertheless, a more immediate and accessible avenue for the transformation of American education is the relationship between the teacher and child. As relationships offer the opportunity for numinous states of being (Corbett, 2012), the relationship between a teacher and a child has this potential.

Mayes describes the teacher-student relationship in the "therapeutic classroom" (2017, p. 26). A foundation stone for the therapeutic classroom is that a teacher engages in "psychospiritual reflectivity" in which she cultivates an inner relationship between the personal self and transpersonal self (Mayes, 2017, p. 55). The teacher can then model that inner relationship with herself in the classroom environment.

Indeed, in *Teaching and Learning for Wholeness*, Mayes describes the "therapeutic classroom" as "an environment for students in which they not only expand cognitively but deepen psychodynamically" (2017, p. 26). According to Mayes, in the therapeutic classroom, the transactional relationship between teacher and student is *mutually* transformative due to the engagement of "deep educational processes" and, citing Salzberger-Wittenberg, "the emotional experience of teaching and learning" (2017, p. 26). The teacher and the learner thus synergistically lead each other in the transformative classroom.

BRING FORTH WHAT IS WITHIN YOU

After helping to lead a child forth from the undifferentiated state to the egoic state of consciousness into a relationship with the outer and inner worlds, the second question arises: "What do we *bring out* from the child?" What we bring out from children requires listening and affirming the experiences that they share. According to Jung, "[w]e do not usually listen to children at any stage of their careers; in all the essentials we treat them as *non compos mentis* and in all the unessentials they are drilled to the perfection of automatons (1954, p. 14).

Is there a way to support ego-development in children's education and not turn them into automatons or "Borg drones?" The key to this dilemma is supporting a child's connection to the archetypal realms of consciousness from which one experiences the *numinous*. Besides nature and relationships, as mentioned already, children and adults experience numinosity in dreams, the body, creativity, and mystical states of unity (Corbett, 2012). One way to retain a child's transpersonal connections in education is to advocate the value for time and engagement of the imagination, the arts, play, and contact with nature. With standardized education, testing, and emphasis on STEM subjects, little time and value are given to soul-care.

I will use an acronym, PAN-I (i.e., play, art, nature, imagination), as a complementary hypothetical formulation juxtaposed to STEM. The "-I" in PAN-I indicates that *Imagination* is ever-present in *Play*, *Art*, and immersion in *Nature*. The "I" also stands for a child's ego-*Identity* that educators are entrusted with nurturing. I suggest PAN-I widens opportunities for a child to build confidence and a sense of identity by painting, playing, or taking care of a vegetable garden. The acronym PAN also refers to the *panoramic* view of a child's whole being that the educational policymakers have lost sight of. I have devised this acronym to call attention to the imbalance in how public schools educate today. It is also an expression of hope for the future of children's education.

I offer a story of my kindergarten experience in contrast to my two grandsons (both were in kindergarten this year) to demonstrate this imbalance. As I have vivid early childhood memories, the images of my kindergarten experiences—decades ago—are surprisingly clear. I remember painting at an easel, finger painting, coloring with crayons, cutting paper and pasting it together, spending time building things with blocks, swinging, sliding, playing in the sandbox, caring for the bunny and the turtle, and playing house in the area designated as the "house" in the classroom. I remember the love and compassion of my teacher Mrs. Frost and her full round figure that enveloped me in hugs, the smell of her perfume wafting through the air as she passed by. I learned to recognize and recite the alphabet, count to ten, identify colors, and tie my shoes. I still have the slip of paper with the star stickers indicating the full spectrum of my kindergarten accomplishments.

On the other hand, near the end of the kindergarten year, my grandsons are sight-reading words, writing sentences, labeling their drawings, counting to one hundred, adding and subtracting. I am a part-time caregiver to one grandson (and two other grandchildren), and due to the COVID-19 pandemic, I witnessed and participated in their virtual education. I can testify that it was a disturbing "forced march" for my grandson, his classmates, and his devoted, talented, and committed teacher to successfully achieve the standardized curriculum's goals. I felt helpless in the dimming light in my grandson's eyes and the unhappy expression of withstanding an intolerable situation during these school days online.

In stark contrast to my grandson's situation, without a STEM education and given my early "PAN-I type" education, I still managed to attend college, receive a master's degree, become a healthcare provider, a tapestry artist, and develop excellent computer skills.

CONCLUSION

Honoring and safeguarding a child's innate capacity for numinous experience is vital for soul-care in children's education. Children's numinous experiences foster inner resiliency of faith, self-discovery, creativity, and psychological well-being.

The sacred duty of educators is to *educate,* which means that teachers lead children as models of faith, exemplifying how to retain a connection to their own souls. As teachers cannot lead a child further than they themselves have been, teachers must explore their own transpersonal realms establishing a resiliency of faith founded on those experiences. In the soul-care of a child, the education offered in American public schools must value, nurture, and preserve the soul light of the numinous seen—in both its primal and transcendent aspects—in the radiant light of joy in a child's eyes.

REFERENCES

Abington Township, Pennsylvania, et al. v. Schempp et al., 374 US 203 (1963).
Agostini et al. v. Felton et al., 117 S. Ct. (1997).
Bernstein, J. S. (2005). *Living in the Borderland: The evolution of consciousness and the challenge of healing trauma.* Routledge.

Block, A. (1997). *I'm only bleeding: Education as the practice of violence against children.* Peter Lang.

Bode, B. (1921). *Fundamentals of education.* McMillan.

Corbett, L. (1996). *The religious function of the psyche.* Routledge.

Corbett, L. (2012). *Psyche and the sacred: Spirituality beyond religion.* Spring Journal.

Crawford, M., & Rossiter, G. (2006). *Reasons for living: Education and young people's search for meaning, identity and spirituality. A handbook.* ACER Press.

Cremin, L. (1988). *American education: The metropolitan experience: 1876–1980.* Harper and Row.

Dewey, J. (1916). *Democracy and education.* Macmillan.

Etymology Online Dictionary (n.d.). Faith. Retrieved November 15, 2021, from https://www.etymonline.com/word/Faith

Etymology Online Dictionary (n.d.). Educate. Retrieved November 15, 2021, from https://www.etymonline.com/word/Educate

Etymology Online Dictionary (n.d.). Religion. Retrieved November 15, 2021, from https://www.etymonline.com/word/Religion

Fordham, M. (1994). *Children as individuals.* Free Association Books.

Hay, D., & Nye, R. (2006). *The spirit of the child.* Jessica Kingsley.

Jung, C. G. (1954). *The development of personality: Papers on child psychology, education, and related subjects* (R. F. C. Hull, Trans.). In H. Read et al. (Eds.), *The collected works of C. G. Jung: Vol. 17.* Princeton University Press.

Jung, C. G. (1969a). *The structure and dynamics of the psyche* (R. F. C. Hull, Trans.). In H. Read et al. (Eds.), *The collected works of C. G. Jung: Vol. 8. Structure and dynamics of the psyche.* Princeton University Press.

Jung, C. G. (1969b). *The archetypes and the collective unconscious* (R. F. C. Hull, Trans.). In H. Read et al. (Eds.), *The collected works of C. G. Jung: Vol. 9.1.* Princeton University Press.

Jung, C. G. (1969c). *Aion: Researches into the phenomenology of the self* (R. F. C. Hull, Trans.). In H. Read et al. (Eds.), *The collected works of C. G. Jung: Vol. 9.2.* Princeton University Press.

Jung, C. G. (1970). *Psychology and religion: West and East* (R. F. C. Hull, Trans.). In H. Read et al. (Eds.), *The collected works of C. G. Jung: Vol. 11.* Princeton University Press.

Jung, C. G. (1971). *Psychological types* (R. F. C. Hull, Trans.). In H. Read et al. (Eds.), *The collected works of C. G. Jung: Vol. 6. Psychological Types.* Princeton University Press.

Jung, C. G. (1977). *The symbolic life* (R. F. C. Hull, Trans.). In H. Read et al. (Eds.), *The collected works of C. G. Jung: Vol.18. The symbolic life* (pp. 267–90). Princeton University Press. (Original work published 1954)

Klein, M. (1975/1932). *The psychoanalysis of children* (Trans. A. Strachey). Delacorte Press.

Lemon v. Kurtzman, 403 U.S. 602 (1971).

Mayes, C. (2004). *Teaching mysteries: Foundations of a spiritual pedagogy.* University Press of America.

Mayes, C. (2005). *Jung and education: Elements of an archetypal pedagogy.* Rowman & Littlefield Education Press.

Mayes, C. (2007). *Inside education: Depth Psychology in teaching and learning.* Atwood Publishing.

Mayes, C. (2010). *A study in Jungian pedagogy: The archetypal hero's journey in teaching and learning.* Atwood Publishing.

Mayes, C. (2016a). *Developing the whole student: New horizons for holistic education.* Rowman & Littlefield Education Press.

Mayes, C. (2016b). *An introduction to the collected works of C. G. Jung: Psyche as spirit.* Rowman & Littlefield Education Press.

Mayes, C. (2017). *Teaching and learning for wholeness: The role of archetypes is educational processes.* Rowman & Littlefield Education Press.

Mayes, C. (2020). *Archetype, culture, and the individual in education: The three pedagogical narratives.* Routledge.

Meyer, M. (trans.). (1984). *The secret teaching of Jesus: Four gnostic gospels.* Random House.

Nixon, G. (1997). American education: Horror experience. *A Journal of Archetype & Culture, 62* (Spring), 55–70.

Palmer, P. (1993). *To know as we are known.* HarperCollins.

Otto, R. (1958). *The idea of the holy.* Oxford University Press.

Progress Report on the Federal Implementation of the STEM Education Strategic Plan (October 2019). Retrieved August 31, 2020 from https://www.whitehouse.gov /wp-content/uploads/2019/10/Progress-Report-on-the-Federal-Implementation-of -the-STEM-Education-Strategic-Plan.pdf

Spring, J. (1976). *Educating the worker-citizen.* Prentice Hall.

Watras, J. (2002). *The foundations of educational curriculum and diversity: 1565 to the present.* Allyn and Bacon.

Wexler, P. (2008). *Symbolic movement: Critique and spirituality of education.* Sense Publishers.

Winnicott, D. W. (1992). *Psychoanalytic explorations.* C. Winnicott, R. Shepherd, & M. Davis (Eds.). Harvard University Press.

Chapter 5

Rehabilitating Echo

Susan Persing

Echo is a mythological figure who rarely makes the shortlist of well-known Greek female characters, divine or mortal. She is seldom discussed apart from her relationships with Narcissus and Pan, and when she is, she is often marginalized as a nymph without any degree of autonomy, a "pathetic push-over" (Chapman, 2010, p. 1). Echo has been seen as manipulative and even calculating. Is this the whole story?

In this chapter, I go beyond conventional views in search of who Echo is at the deepest level. There is more to her than meets the eye. Echo may be a virgin, but she is pregnant with hermeneutic potential. She is voluble but silenced, eloquent but mute, outrageously wounded yet salvific; she is one of the most paradoxical figures in Greek mythology and one of its most curiously potent.

What is Echo's essential nature? Is she good or bad? How has the curse inflicted on her by Hera influenced the development and understanding of expressive language, from birth to adulthood? What does it mean to echo? What is echoing? What is the significance of the myth in modern terms? Finally, what are Echo's redeeming qualities, if any? How might she inform the modern psyche?

As I move along in this chapter, I will note parallels with Mayes's (2020) archetypal pedagogy. The idea is to show another aspect of Echo's character and impact—namely, her role as a teacher in enacting what it means, at the profoundest levels, not only to teach but also to learn. Additionally, this exercise contributes to archetypal pedagogy's attempt to uncover the archetypal core of teaching and learning.

ECHO'S ESSENTIAL NATURE

One day, a nymph named Echo is frolicking in the woods when she comes across the great god Zeus in mid-dalliance with a nymph. As she quickly exits the scene, Echo runs into Hera, Zeus's watchful and jealous wife, who is searching for him, suspecting that he is once again consorting with nymphs. Echo delays Hera with idle chatter, giving Zeus and his lover a chance to escape discovery. Hera is furious and unleashes her anger on Echo, punishing her by taking away her ability to form her own words. All Echo can do is compulsively repeat the words of others in her vicinity.

So goes the popular retelling of the myth by D'Aulaire and D'Aulaire (1962) featuring Echo as the love interest of the great nature god Pan. In this version, Echo is ebullient and talkative, rarely pausing to catch her breath. Try as he might, Pan could not catch her attention or win her affection with either music or poetry; she had lost her heart to another.

Echo next appears in pursuit of the young Narcissus. The nearer she comes to the handsome god, the more Echo is inflamed with love for the object of her passion. Narcissus, however, does not seem to notice her as he has become mesmerized (cursed by Nemesis) by his reflection in a still pool of water. Echo takes advantage of Narcissus's words of love to his reflection: "I love you." Cursed by Hera to only repeat the words of Narcissus, Echo proceeds to do what her name implies. In a failed communication that often happens between potential lovers, Echo's repetition suggests that Narcissus means something he doesn't, and Echo is rejected out of hand. Heartsick and forlorn, she can only watch as Narcissus, captivated by his own reflection and unable to tear himself away from the water's edge, dies. Defeated and ashamed, Echo eventually solidifies until she becomes like a rock, an inanimate hardness doomed to endlessly reflect the voice of the Other.

Acoustic and Reverberating Echoes

So goes the story of Echo. But to fully understand her, one must also consider the physical phenomena she came to produce. An *acoustic echo* is "the repetition of a sound by the reflection of sound waves from a solid surface that reaches the ear at least one-fifteenth of a second after the original sound" (Hollander, 1981, p. 1). In contrast to the acoustic echo, a *reverberating echo* prolongs rather than repeats the original sound. The sound echoed back depends upon the shape and texture of the surroundings onto which the original is projected. A flat, smooth surface will return sound differently from a curved or porous one. The original sound is lost upon its projection and is rescued by the echo, which returns the origin to itself but is at the same time an original source of sound in itself (Hollander, 1981, p. 1).

So it is also with teaching and learning. For, as Mayes (2017) insists, there is inevitably a gap between what the teacher wishes to be teaching and what the student actually and ultimately hears. Here we must turn to depth educational theory, which, drawing upon Freudian, post-Freudian (Britzman, 2011) as well as Jungian and post-Jungian theory (Mayes, 2020), is the attempt to get an ever deeper purchase on what is going on inside the teacher and student in the many processes and interactions that make up the educational endeavor. These efforts comprise the nascent subdiscipline of educational psychology called depth educational psychology.

In the present case, we are dealing with what depth educational psychology has termed the "subjective curriculum." As opposed to the official curriculum that is devised and issued by the state, the subjective curriculum is each learner's reaction to that curriculum. Each student's subjective curriculum is shaped by neurological, psychodynamic, familial, cultural, and even ethico-spiritual reasons. In addition, the teacher's and student's personal interaction—mostly involving mutual projections—will come into play. Taking the mythological view of these phenomena deepens our views of education at the same time as it makes actual the myths we unconsciously live by.

An echo cannot produce sound without the origin, but waves are returned as an echo; that echo has an identity of its own. The boundary between the original sound and its repetition is blurred; they are separate phenomena that exist in dialectic relation to each other. Echo's voice is thus heard only in the distorted voice of Narcissus that her repetition produces, but it does not stop there. In this lies Echo's survival, and arguably, her triumph. The educational ramifications of this will emerge in due course.

THE HISTORICAL ECHO

Echo appears in many historical sources but is best known in the story of Echo and Pan, which appears in Longus's tale of Daphnis and Chloe (Longus, 1956/1956–2004), and Echo and Narcissus from Mandelbaum's translation of Ovid's Metamorphosis (Ovid, 1993). Ovid's tale is dated to 43 BCE to 17–18 CE, nearly two centuries before Longus takes up the narrative, yet Longus relates the tale as if it took place long before Ovid's time and gives it its appearance of antiquity.

Although Echo is associated with Pan in various textual fragments throughout antiquity, an original narrative that unifies the textual fragments is nowhere to be found. Longus unites the fragments in his narrative and creates a fictional myth-making event. Longus echoes Echo and reveals her as "a presence that is simultaneously absent. . . . The absent Echo becomes the absent object, whose presence is perceptual but not actual" (Chapman, 2010, p. 2). She becomes a way of seeing rather than an object that is seen and questions the perception of language and challenges its fixed meaning. In Echo's case, it is the person who takes on increasing ethical heft.

In other historical accounts, Echo appears as part of the natural landscape. In Elizabethan version of the tale, Echo's dismembered limbs continue to sing even as they are torn apart. There is an intimate connection between Echo's body (which includes matter and earth) and her echoic song. In Apuleius's mention of Echo in *The Golden Ass* (Apuleius, 1994), she appears with Pan, echoing the sounds of nature, while Pan consoles the banished Psyche. Chapman (2010) suggests that Echo's role in witnessing Psyche's distress and echoing back to her the sounds of nature represents an attempt to ease the suffering brought about by Psyche's separation from nature.

ECHO WITH PAN, ECHO WITH NARCISSUS: A COMPARISON

Echo's relationships in the myths as told by Longus and Ovid reveal different aspects of her. In the myth with Pan, Echo's mother is a nymph, but her father is a mortal. Her dual parentage enables her to inhabit worlds above and below. She is closely associated with grounded, natural elements and loves music, yet her echoic voice is ethereal, untethered, and otherworldly. When appearing with Narcissus, she has a determined and willful nature and is pictured as cunning, manipulative, and persuasive.

Hollander (1981) states, "If Pan's Echo is lyric, Narcissus' is satiric" (p. 12). She is "a powerful mocker" with a "way of deconstructing words" (pp. 11–12). Cursed to repeat language, Echo communicates by emphasizing and repeating word fragments, for instance, repeating only the ends of phrases. She can reinterpret through inflection and thereby create new meaning or intent. In Ovid's tale (Ovid, 1993), for instance, Echo snares Narcissus by repeating his own words. Thinking that he is talking to a person in the woods, Narcissus calls out,

> "Let's meet." And with the happiest of reply that ever was to leave her lips, she cries; "Let's meet"; then, seconding her words, she rushed out of the woods, that she might fling her arms around the neck she longed to clasp. (Ovid, 1993, p. 92)

Echo manipulates the words to change their intent; Narcissus is trying to find his friends while Echo has engineered what she hopes will be a romantic rendezvous. Echo thus employs a rhetoric of recursiveness and indirection, which helps examine intellectually, psychologically, and spiritually complex matters that simple linearity cannot capture and often misrepresents.

Training in the Service of the Sign versus Education in the Service of the Symbol

In educational terms, this difference in the curriculum between simple and even simplistic linearity, on one hand, and a psychologically and existentially complex presentation of rich material that requires the student's complex appropriation of the subject matter, on the other hand, is what Mayes calls "training in the service of the sign" versus "education in the spirit of the symbol," respectively (2016). It is the latter that Jung most approved of, and it is the latter—namely, education in the spirit of the symbol—in Echo's rhetoric of recursiveness and indirection that is essential to how symbols operate but is anathema to the sign. Mayes is worth citing at length on this topic since it points to both the "Echo-like" quality of every teacher who situates herself in the domain of the symbol in her teaching, and the "teacher-like" qualities of Echo by way of her uses of language. Mayes (2016, p. 194) writes,

> In Training in the Service of the Sign, the teacher more or less mechanistically transmits an "official curriculum," determined by the state, which, however much she may or may not agree with it, she has had little or no role in creating. . . . Standardized tests [become] the major means of enforcing the official curriculum. . . . Teacher and student are not called upon to choose or change in any core ways under the ethical pull of a true existential gravity in the classroom. [Conversely, in the service of the symbol] the curriculum has the potential to be a living thing because, like the symbol itself, it is an occasion for *I-Thou* relationships to form as individuals join to generate multi-dimensional interpretations, which each student may then appropriate in his own way in the furtherance of his unique life-narrative as it proceeds on the road to individuation. . . . Training in the Service of the Sign, in its rigidity and anonymity, is atomistic, anti-narratival. Education in the Spirit of the Symbol, in its multi-perspectival nature, its dynamism, its organic malleability to change to fit the changing needs and moods of the class, and its focus upon individual interpretation, is holistic and narratival.

We need Echo, Chapman writes, because "without Echo's reverberations the psyche becomes transfixed, with no other reflection than its own" (Chapman, 2010, p. 263). When Echo is spurned, as Narcissus knows only too well, it can lead to death. His final words to Echo, "I'd sooner die than say I'm yours!" (Ovid, 1993, p. 92), proved prophetic. Yet, ironically, the reflecting mirror makes Narcissus more aware of the unknown Other staring back at him from the water's reflective surface.

THE ARCHETYPAL ECHO/ECHO AS A
LIMINAL AND INTERMEDIARY FIGURE

Intermediacy is the defining characteristic of Echo in both primary myths, according to Chapman (2010). She serves as a bridge not only between contrasting elements in the two myths but also between self and Other. Inhabiting "a place between presence and absence" (Greenberg, 1998, p. 326), she inhabits the space between speech and intention, and between image and sound. It is possible, Chapman notes, that Echo is present wherever fragmented voice, reverberating sound, meandering repetition, and diversionary reflections appear.

Echo's character includes aspects of liminality. Liminality, described by Turner (1987), is a place that is betwixt and between, neither here nor there, "a realm of pure possibility whence novel configurations of ideas and relations may arise" (p. 7). Echo thus operates at the threshold of experience. She is less obvious than Hermes, who travels directly between worlds. In contrast, as a nymph and liminal figure, Echo fuses divine and earthly aspects to connect the present with the past and self with others. She is seen to play with language, interpretation, and meaning (Kalsched, 1996) to reveal previously unknown faces to the objects she reflects through her repetition of their independent speech.

Insofar as the teacher is urging transformation in her students, she is necessarily inviting them into a liminal space. This is a transitional area, a psychospiritual venue, into which they morph and move after they have transcended the *anomie* of the corporate system (which the educational system both wittingly and unwittingly serves) but before they have coalesced into a new identity, one that is more suited to their now more complex, more nuanced identity—rich with novel ethical and spiritual possibilities.

Because Echo both repeats sound and reflects images, she moves images from unconscious to conscious awareness. Hera intends to punish Echo through the curse she inflicts on her. At first blush, Hera seems to have wrought a fine vengeance. And yet, at the same time, her curse also positions Echo to play an intermediary role that does not so much catch Echo in a trap between "being and nothingness" (Sartre, 2006) as it enshrines her there. Her persistent voice in the absence of physical substance qualifies her as another of humanity's sacred translators of silence into significance and abandonment into advocacy.

Echo also becomes a "consort of history," by creating and signaling human memory. Her echo preserves experience within the earth; it returns the voice of experience to the speaker in the form of memory. She can alter the meaning of words, thereby "assisting in the creation of satire, fiction, irony, and history" (Chapman, 2010, p. 124). Like Hermes, she is a messenger and communicator, but her role is less obvious, oblique, and can be used to recreate reality. Like a prism, what passes through her can be distorted. In Chapman's words, "Echo has graduated to the archetypal. . . . She has transformed from being a source of echoing to actually becoming the echo. She is not only alive in the act of reflecting, but she is also the act of reflecting" (Chapman, 2010, pp. 63–64). Perhaps, as Chapman muses, Hera's curse contains a hidden gift that allows Echo to access her inner wisdom through compulsive repetition.

ECHO AS THERAPIST

Echo is a good listener. In this way, she might also appear as a psychotherapist or function like one. What is the primary task of a therapist but to reflect the laments, contradictions, or longings of one seeking recognition and reconciliation with self and Others? Echo is embodied whenever one feels unheard, invisible, or caught in a "compulsive repetition." This reinforces Kalsched's idea that at the heart of many conventional "disorders" is an archetypal mythical core (Kalsched, 1996).

In therapeutic terms, Echo challenges the transcendence of the usual therapeutic project of shaping the client's consciousness according to predetermined categories of "health," such as the ability to return to work or adapt to norms. Echo is more than that. She aids in empowering the client, in freedom, to forge the unique contours of her own phenomenological universe using proximity and the surrounding landscape to add emphasis or nuance to what she echoes back (Slife, 1993), precisely the role of the existentially authentic teacher in Mayes's (2012) view. Perhaps in Echo's company, as in the company of any great teacher, one hears the voice of the heart for the first time in her echo. At any rate, it is becoming clear that among Echo's broad range of talents and capacities, the role of the teacher is one of the most evident and efficacious.

Echo teaches autonomy even in the face of her limitations. Here, in this engagingly obscure genealogy of a myth, art does not imitate life by mirroring life as expected. It is not what Rorty has called "the mirror of nature" (Rorty, 2009). Rather, the piece of art generates myths about its own origin that occlude as much as they reveal. The same may be said of Echo's echoing. Echo's echoes *objectively reproduce* what they *receive*. Yet, they do so with such subtle variations in ethical volume and emotional timbre that Echo is commenting a great deal more than she is copying.

Under the naturopathic principle that "like cures like" and the commonsense notion that one cannot offer authentic empathy without being wounded and experiencing the pain oneself, the complete Jungian therapist is a "wounded healer." As a therapist, Echo, too, is wounded but also transformed into a compassionate healer. She is also a hook for projection. What is a projection, however, except a psychic echo of someone's deep desire? Echo mirrors back these desires with an invitation to integrate them as part of oneself.

Echo is thus doubly an echo. It requires steady, sober self-reflection on her part to resist hungrily consuming the other's projection and then counter-projecting her own needs. Rather, she instead echoes back the other's tumult, poignancy, unrest, or apathy so that the other is seen and held. Yet Echo's echoes can subtly transform the other's original plaint through her witness and reflection so that, upon hearing herself or himself, the other hears something different, possibly more dynamic. This is the purpose of therapy, according to Jung: not to be happier necessarily, but to be more creative and compassionate in one's situation. Jung was stoic in the presence of psychopathology and recognized in the language of pathology a lament and desire of the soul to be present, to be witnessed, and to heal. A certain stoicism, a creative resignation, in the face of her fate is what turns Echo's punishment by Hero into a higher calling as hermeneut and therapist.

ECHO IN MODERNITY

It is easy to find contemporary parallels to the myth of Echo and Narcissus. We know Echo as the scholar silenced in the halls of academia and denied advancement, reduced to repeating the formulations of more senior colleagues in their native language. Deprived by culture and tradition of the agency of her own words and perspective, she speaks in a foreign language that denies the full expression of her being.

Echo pops up unexpectedly in other modern-day situations. For example, she accompanies the woman or man with a narcissistic partner, a relationship that can only be maintained by echoing the other's words, ideas, and interests, desperately hoping the relationship can graduate to love. Eventually, the desperate desire to be heard is forfeited, and the scorned lover shatters into just fragments of her former self—like pebbles and shards, which, as an amplified image, symbolize the voice and ambition of the unresponsive loved one.

Davis (2005) finds many similarities between the myth of Echo and Narcissus and the biblical story of Sampson and Delilah. He uses both tales to amplify a psychological phenomenon he calls echoing. In each case, the relationship between lovers can only survive when the echoing partner gives up her or his own passions and becomes resigned to mimic the partner's language and interests. The echoing partner forfeits her agency out of fear of losing the relationship, as when the narcissistic lover hurls projections of blame onto the echoing partner or leaves when his or her demands are not met. This unfortunate situation inevitably leads to the death of the partnership for both parties involved. It is crucial, Davis concludes, to understand that narcissism and echoing go hand in hand.

In a rarely cited essay, "Marriage as a Psychological Relationship" (Hull, 2014), Jung opined that marriage begins with a nexus of projections of each partner on to the other. Each partner has a specific idea of who they are falling in love with. Partners may not know that the idea of who their beloved is has less to do with the actual qualities of the person and are more likely the result of what they project onto the other—the unconscious ideals or unclaimed aspects of their inner reality. These projections can be both positive and negative. One can be either repelled or attracted by unintegrated aspects of themselves. Images of the ideal partner hang in mid-air and beckon to be realized in a living person. As Jung observes, "Projections change the world into the replica of one's unknown face" (Jung, 1968, p. 9). Eventually, projection creates an illusory relationship instead of a real one and isolates the lover from the beloved.

Echo can teach us a bit about projection. Echo's troubles with Narcissus began in the throes of a passionate projection, hers onto him, his in the reflecting pond where Echo became the reflective hook for that projection. Perhaps Echo lacked the beauty or self-confidence she saw in Narcissus. Perhaps Narcissus was repelled or even attracted by the desperate quality of Echo's pursuit. This is relevant for modern relationships as well.

Jung advises that for a marriage not only to last but also result in psychological growth, each partner must withdraw his or her initial projections onto the other. Those projections, to be sure, fed the flames of the initial passion and were subsequently sanctified (and sublimated) in the solemnity of a marriage vow. To the extent that each partner can withdraw their projections to see and love the other for who they really are, they not only solidify their marriage but come closer to the great desideratum of the Jungian project: individuation. Individuation is in one sense tantamount to the withdrawal of projections and recognizing oneself as the source of these projections, especially their contradictions, and integrating their dialectical energy toward the ongoing growth of the soul and the betterment of one's culture.

The concept of echoing is also an important developmental step in the acquisition of language (Davis, 2005). We learn to speak by repeating back what we have heard from our parents and caregivers. Eventually, as neurological development proceeds, we assimilate the implied meanings of the words and use them to formulate independent speech, giving voice to our unique thoughts and desires. This is not only a crucial developmental step but the basis for memory and rational thought. This capacity for structural echoing seems to be genetically inherited and familiar. An instinctual drive, repetition is an essential mechanism that drives normative development and the ability to relate to others.

Echoing is also critical to the transition from a state of primary narcissism—defined as an early stage of childhood development in which the libido is directed toward the developing ego—to the ability to establish interpersonal relationships, the formation of object-relatedness. This happens as the infant echoes and imitates his parents, then eventually sees himself or herself as a separate being in relation to others (Davis, 2005). This early developmental process is reflected in both Echo and Narcissus, echoing and narcissism, creating a clearer picture of the relationship between self and Other. Echo seems to hold the missing piece. Her echoing, the repetition of the speech of others, reveals self to Other and Other to self.

REHABILITATING ECHO

Is it possible, then, to find a new angle or interpretation of Echo's myth that restores her agency and power in the face of her undeniable handicap via Hera? Käll provides an interesting perspective, arguing, "Echo's words cannot be reduced to a simple repetition of a clear and distinct original. . . . Echo's voice is a disruption of the words she repeats, and each repetition is also its own origin" (Käll, 2015, p. 59). Echo makes her voice present as something new. Echo's handicap is not so much her lack of a voice, but rather her lack of unbound origin. Unable to originate sound, she remains mute but for her act of repetition. It is her act of repetition that reclaims her voice.

Is Echo a passive victim of Hera's jealousy? Hannan (1992) argues that Echo is not the weak and hapless victim popular imagination has portrayed her to be. Not only does she take care of herself, but she is also a shrewd observer who opportunistically preys on the object of her affections. Hannan writes, "Echo's very nature is parasitic; she must form her speech from the words of others" (1992, p. 6). Hannan notes that while Echo's responses appear to be empathetic to Narcissus, she ignores his feelings and acts out of her own self-interest. She has in fact created the Narcissus she loves at first sight out of whole cloth; he is an image of her imagination.

Completely identified with the object of her fantasy, she pursues him relentlessly with no empathy for his feelings. When he rejects her, it only increases her desire for him. She is unable to see his point of view; she feels a deep sense of shame when her desires are frustrated by his rejection. Her fatal compulsion continues to burn and is eventually turned inward toward herself; she becomes withered and dried and eventually dies.

Although not a protagonist, Echo facilitates origination elsewhere. Her clever manipulation of repeated words points to the creative potential inherent in words themselves. Echo's grievous injury, inflicted by Hera, took away her ability to speak for herself, to present herself in words of her own choice. She can only echo the narcissism of her lover in an attempt to make herself an object of his love. In contrast, Narcissus was merely in love with his reflection, oblivious to Echo's passions.

Echo is bound to repeat the words of her lover, but Narcissus's words also express her own desire and need. Simple repetition thus becomes ambiguous. Despite being cursed to echo others, she is not limited to merely repeating Narcissus in an unambiguous manner. Her voice "emerges as an origin in and through its echo" (Käll 2015, p. 61). What she lacks in independent origin she makes up for in creating and inflecting new and altered meanings. In her repetition, the voice of Narcissus is transformed.

Like Echo's pursuit of Narcissus, this repetition creates a kind of psychic tension that is also creative. "The psyche is in this way an artist—a shaper, maker, a creator of beauty within itself" (Berry, 1982, p. 113). Unlike Narcissus, who attempted to live simply by keeping his identity and subjectivity free from the complicating echoes of his surroundings, Echo was unable to live without his originating sound to shape her self-identity through repeating his voice, using her surroundings to shape and alter the meanings of his words and craft a reflecting consciousness.

Echo's passion, her compulsion, is painful to her because her longing cannot be fulfilled. Her love requires distance from her chosen one; without this space, the echo cannot sound, and she has no voice. Proximity to her lover verges on containment in him (Hull, 2014), in his words, which she cannot nuance through her repetition. Silenced through closeness, she betrays the reflective capacity that distance provides yet suffers at a distance because her lover is forever unattainable. Echo's distance creates space for beauty and creativity to appear. In the same way, psychic distance must be cultivated in order to hear the soul's self-reflective capacity. Being contained within the Self without an ego identity silences the dialectic between the ego as *related* to Self and the recognition of Self *as* Other.

Berry, with perhaps an oblique nod in the direction of Freud's "repetition compulsion," points out that Echo's penchant for repetition is a possible "attempt at continuity" (2017, p. 110), an effort to rework concepts or ideas, to bring them to awareness and take them to heart. Though repetition may appear superficial, it can also point to a deeper longing for self-reflection. We repeat what we wish to make real and, in some way, concrete. Echo's attraction to Narcissus is not an attraction of opposites but that of a pair: they are "of the same essential nature" (Berry, 2017, p. 113). This similarity implies that we tend to echo what is like us, and "within one's echoing is a kind of self" (Berry, 2017, p. 113). Perhaps through the echoing, we find what we desire is in fact the relationship with the parts of ourselves we have lost through projection onto the speaking object.

Echo also challenges the postmodern critique that scholarly discourse is an involuted even incestuous structure of commentators commenting on each other in a prestigious and self-celebratory game of mutual legitimation. Seen from Echo's point of view, each scholar echoes issues of long-standing importance in a way that both acknowledges the past and encourages innovative perspectives.

In a similar figure, the great teacher, in her curricular considerations and instructional goals, neither remains fixated on the putative glories of the past nor is he dazzled by the promised panaceas of the future. He sees the need to anchor the discourse of the classroom in healthy respect for tried-and-true canonical knowledge that forms the foundations and provides the parameters that make not only the discourse in a discipline but the discipline itself possible. This balancing of the classical impulse, which is directed toward the maintenance of culture, and the Romantic impulse, which strives after new individual expression, often in radical critique of that culture, is central to the memorable teacher's *modus operandi*.

Like the teacher, Echo thus becomes a practitioner of the art of hermeneutics. Hermeneutics, simply, is the art of interpretation and has as its goal to understand a text or situation and to be understood (Zimmermann, 2015). The hermeneut interprets texts as part of a greater or meaningful whole. This is what is meant by the term *hermeneutic circle*. The hermeneutic circle implies reflection, the ability to hear, read, and process the ideas of others. As ideas linger in the space between the initial hearing and the scholar's reflection, they become subtly nuanced through interaction with the specific contours of the scholar's psychic landscape. What emerges through distance, reverberation, and time is something perceptibly original–new knowledge. Echo is an integral part of this hermeneutic circle, and her role in it is manifestly pedagogical.

CONCLUDING THOUGHTS

Echo's transformation from a chatterbox to an echoing nymph was Hera's way of punishing what she considered deceptive and seductive speech. As a result, Echo was given voice only in response to others. At this point in the story, she is not left completely without agency, however. She still retains her bodily form and apparently can choose to withdraw from the company of others and remain silent. She is, therefore, able to exercise her will and desires. Her desire is what drives her to pursue Narcissus. Her mobility allows her to inflect her responses, imparting meaning to the Other through the echo of their words. She can use the surrounding landscapes to further alter the meaning of the phrases she repeats.

Echo undergoes a second transformation after the death of Narcissus when her body withers away and becomes a stone. As a solid surface without agency or will that continues to repeat the words of others, she loses the boundaries of her physical body and her individual identity. While after the first transformation she retained her body and limited creative agency, after the second transformation, she loses her mobility, therefore cannot escape, and must compulsively repeat all sounds in her vicinity. And yet, Ovid (1993) tells us that the power of sound continues to live within Echo. Echo's disembodied speech, free of boundaries, becomes a form of reflective consciousness.

Echo's first transformation binds her tongue but situates her in the surrounding world in relation to others. Her second transformation does not signal a complete obliteration by death. Rather, behind the hardness of her stone façade, she reflects and brings to life the voices of others. She lives on as long as she receives their sound. Like the notion of *kenosis* in Christian theology—Christ's "emptying of himself" to become a servant to all—Echo goes through a similar process, giving her a whisper of messianic potential. She stands between that which is known and not known, between confident hope and existential despair. Caught between the constant action and exasperating invisibility of *Deus absconditus* in our lives, a savior-like Echo intervenes. As the avatar of the transcendent, her very presence is a constant reminder of what we cannot yet grasp.

There is a great deal to learn from this complicated nymph whose story reverberates through time. She is multivalent, as are all figures of Greek mythology, but her polysemous nature, fructifying in the form of intriguing new questions, makes her all the more generative in a scholarly sense. She also brings matters of existential importance to life, which is not a triumph of certitude but a trek into questions of increasing complexity and charm. Such also is the calling of the great teacher. It thus becomes not only possible but necessary to see Echo in her pedagogical aspect as one of the most important of her manifestations to us.

Echo's repetitions are more than repetitions, for they also contain reflective listening and nuanced critical commentary, key elements of the hermeneutic circle. She blazes trails of phenomenological adventure and cuts out large swathes of space relating to voice, body, and consciousness. Through her ongoing recovery and discovery of teleological hope and innate goodness, Echo terraforms her initial landscape of woundedness and loss into a surprising new Eden of wonderment and lyricism. She is thus not only a teacher but a teacher *par excellence.*

Maybe it's time to move Echo to the A-list.

REFERENCES

Apuleius. (1994). *The golden ass* (P. Walsh, Trans.). Oxford University Press.

Berger, A.-E. (1996). The latest word from Echo. *New Literary History, 27*(4), 621–41. https://doi.org/10.1353/nlh.1996.0043

Berry, P. (1982). *Echo's subtle body: Contributions to an archetypal psychology*. Spring Publications.

Chapman, L. M. (2010). Revisioning Echo: The mythical figure of Echo and her importance to clinical depth psychology (9781303130311) [Doctoral dissertation, Pacifica Graduate Institute]. Proquest.

Claremont de Castillejo, I. (1997). *Knowing woman: A feminine psychology*. Shambhala.

D'Aulaire, I., & D'Aulaire, E. P. (1962). *Book of Greek myths*. Random House Children's Books.

Davis, D. (2005). Echo in the darkness. *Psychoanalytic Review, 92*(1), 137–51. https://doi.org/10.1521/prev.92.1.137.58711

Greenberg, J. (1998). The echo of trauma and the trauma of Echo. *American Imago, 55*, 319–347.

Hannan, M. (1992). A psychoanalytic interpretation of Ovid's myth of Narcissus and Echo. *Psychoanalytic Review, 79*(4), 555–75. https://web-b-ebscohost-com.pgi.idm .oclc.org/ehost/detail/detail?vid=1&sid=3ad3c216-5e3a-461a-bea9-669901d88041 %40pdc-v-sessmgr01&bdata=JnNpdGU9ZWhvc3QtbGl2ZSZzY29wZT1zaXRl #AN=1993-28805-001&db=psyh

Hollander, J. (1981). *The figure of Echo: A mode of allusion in Milton and after*. University of California Press.

Hull, R. F. C. (Ed.). (2014). VIII. Marriage as a Psychological Relationship. In C. G. H. Jung, *Collected Works of C. G. Jung, Volume 17: Development of Personality* (pp. 187–202). Princeton University Press. https://doi.org/10.1515 /9781400850839–010https://www.overdrive.com/search?q=EA3D9EB7–5F6F -4B49-B533-3D3D42BCA61B

Jung, C. G. (1968). Aion: Researches into the phenomenology of the self. In H. Read, M. S. Fordham, G. Adler, & W. McGuire (Eds.), & R. F. C. Hull (Trans.), *The collected works of C. G. Jung* (2nd ed., Vol. 9ii). Princeton University Press.

Jung, C. G. (2014). *Collected works of C. G. Jung, Volume 6: Psychological types* (R. F. Hull, Ed.). Princeton University Press. https://doi.org/10.1515/9781400850860

Käll, L. F. (2015, February 13). A voice of her own? Echo's own echo. *Continental Philosophy Review, 48*(1), 59–75. https://doi.org/10.1007/s11007-014-9317-x

Kalsched, D. (1996). *The inner world of trauma: Archetypal defenses of the personal spirit*. Routledge.

Kohut, H., & Wolf, E. S. (1978). The disorders of the self and their treatment: An outline. *The International Journal of Psychoanalysis, 59*(4), 413–25.

Lockhart, R. A. (1983). *Words as eggs: Psyche in language and clinic*. Spring.

Longus. (1956–2004). *Daphnis and Chloe* (P. Turner, Trans.). Prestel. (Original work published 1956)

Mayes, C. (2012). *Inside education: Depth Psychology in teaching and learning.* Atwood Publishing.

Mayes, C. (2016). Some Educational Implications of Jung's View of the Sign and the Symbol. *Psychological Perspectives: A Quarterly Journal of Jungian Thought, 59*(2), 191–201.

Mayes, C. (2017). *Teaching and Learning for Wholeness: The role of archetypes in educational processes.* Rowman and Littlefield.

Mayes, C. (2020). *Archetype, culture, and the individual in education: The three pedagogical narratives.* Routledge.

Merleau-Ponty, M. (2012). *Phenomenology of perception* (1st ed.). Routledge.

Mogenson, G. (1992). *Greeting the angels: An imaginal view of the mourning process.* Baywoop.

Ovid. (1993). *The metamorphosis of Ovid* (A. Mandelbaum, Trans.). Harcourt. (Original work published ca. 43 B.C.E to 17 or 18 A.C.E.)

Rorty, R. (2009). *Philosophy and the mirror of nature.* Princeton University Press.

Sartre, J.-P. (2006). *Being and nothingness: An essay on phenomenological ontology.* Routledge.

Slife, B. D. (1993). *Time and psychological explanation.* State University of New York Press.

Turner, V. (1987). Betwixt and between: The liminal period in rites of passage. In L. C. Mahdi, S. Foster, & M. Little (Eds.), *Betwixt and between: Patterns of masculine and feminine initiation.* Open Court.

Zimmermann, J. (2015). Hermeneutics: A very short introduction. https://www.overdrive.com/search?q=EA3D9EB7-5F6F-4B49-B533-3D3D42BCA61B

Chapter 6

Divination, Prophecy, and Revelation as Educative Synchronicities

Vanessa Jankowski

A synchronistic analysis of apocalyptic myths from three different traditions reveals many useful themes in assessing major current global, climatic, and sociopolitical issues as essentially educative ones. In doing this, I will be viewing the topical issue the backdrop of its eternal archetypal infrastructure. Using the work of C. G. Jung and other depth psychologists to discuss symbols, meaning, and synchronicity, this analysis thus explores the archetype from the point of view of archetypal astrology, Hopi mythology, and the Christian Book of *Revelations* to make it clear that (1) although these three perspectives have little in common at the surface level, at the level of the deeply archetypal, which is to say that at their ontological core, they are strikingly similar; (2) the archetypal points of similarity provide referential points along the path of the dominant paradigm changing during an educative process; and (3) this pattern serves an educative purpose for the members of the society from which the myth has emerged.

Apocalyptic mythologies included describe shifts in the dominant cultural paradigms, not the literal ending of the planet's ability to support life. The interpretation of the myths through a symbolic lens reveals synchronicities both within the themes of the mythologies, in that they align with each other, as well as with current world events. As synchronicities readily occur around the constellation of archetypes, these mythologies may be present to draw the collective attention to the psychological transformation and archetypal changes occurring on a collective level. As such, the constellations of archetypes and their corresponding archetypal configurations of synchronicities may serve a prophetic educational function for the landscapes of a culture and provide at least some sense of how and when these changes will take place.

In brief, these inner and outer constellations, meeting the alchemical criterion "As above, so below; as within, so without," educate a people as to who they are as a people and what they can become. They thus serve hortatory and predictive educative functions for a people regarding their individual psychic and collective ideological processes.

Indeed all great teaching can be seen as at its core if we understand the word in its etymological origin as a revelation, as something or someone revealing their deep nature. Huebner thus declares that apocalyptic teaching is that which leads the student to cast off illusions about something and to see it, as far as is possible, for what it is (1999). Apocalyptic teaching is the fulfillment of a teacher's destiny. In contrast, teaching that is simply by rote, standardized, uncritical, and finally, therefore, not educational at all but dull and insipid, bores the students into compliance with the system in which he is trapped. That kind of anti-teaching to students who are being alternated lulled and intimidated into emotional, political, ethical, and spiritual submission and a vast emptiness. Such non-teaching, Huebner (1999) calls mere "idle talk," the pseudo-discourse of an intellectually, ethically, and spiritually bankrupt pedagogy, as in B. F. Skinner's 1968 *The Technology of Teaching.*

SYNCHRONICITIES AND MYTHOLOGY

C. G. Jung (1960) defined synchronicities as meaningful coincidences. Cambray (2009) further clarifies Jung's ideas by describing synchronicities as external events in Newtonian space, which happen in parallel to internal or psychological states. The events have a meaningful connection and provide deeper understanding to the psychic state (Cambray, 2009). Using these definitions and descriptions, I will show how the three mythologies are synchronistically tied to each and to current events. They educate a people into who they are and where they are going in a way that is invested with a numinosity that can only be attributed to the action of the Divine in their collective history. This then becomes a part of their individual history as well (Mayes, 2020).

Keiron Le Grice (2010, p. 121) discusses how synchronicities can be omens "heralding the beginning of a course of action or a critical moment of decisions." In this instance, the synchronicities are the heralding from multiple prophecies and mythologies depicting an apocalypse; that is to say, a collective, archetypal, external, and psychological shift. Marie-Louise Von Franz says archetypes are what underlie the mythology and sciences of a people (1992, p.11). She continues to say that synchronicities occur around the constellation of an archetype (Von Franz, 1992). This offers a theoretical explanation for the synchronistic aligning of these external events and the astrological changes depicted in multiple prophesies.

The Hopi and Christian prophecies emerged thousands of years ago. Originating over 2,000 years ago, astrology described the zodiac signs within the stars and used them to designate Aions during Babylonian times. For these three drastically different groups to align, there must have been a constellation of an archetype drawing forth the synchronicities. Le Grice says this archetypal shift is the collective evolving along the individuation path, becoming more in touch with the Self, the Gods (2010, pp.15 and 45). In this way, the evolution/education of the collective and of the individual are synergistically linked. He says the trial of our time is our need for collective guidance just at the point we have lost our dominant Christian mythology (Le Grice, 2010).

As synchronicities aid the individuation process by drawing consciousness to the transpiring event, the aligning themes within the mythologies may ultimately provide some measure of this needed guidance. As Le Grice references Joseph Campbell's work with mythology, he points to myths as a place to find such guidance (Le Grice, 2010). This raises the question as to which myths are adequate for this task to educate an individual and her culture into not only the need to evolve but also the ways to do it. I suggest the myths discussed here offer such psychological and pedagogical guidance. Jung says the archetypes depicted in changing Aions astrological signs show these needed changes. If other mythologies, from different traditions, include similar points, the overlapping areas reveal the points of greatest archetypal significance. There are more prophecies and mythologies regarding apocalypse, but these three are among those with extensive detailed records and are commonly known.

ARCHETYPES, QUANTUM PHYSICS, AND DEPTH PSYCHOLOGY

The archetypes, which I am referencing here, are the deep, energetic, patterns of the psyche that influence the universe. The archetype *per se* is unknowable and needs an archetypal symbol or image to be apperceived. Deities or mythological figures are one type of archetypal image and their mythology is a description of the characteristics and movements of that archetype. Moreover, these archetypes can be defined as Jung did, as mode of perceptions, to gain awareness of the archetypal psyche. This capacity to be aware of the archetype separate from the person is that which made Jung a great clinician. He

was able to deeply listen to the ontologically reality of the archetypal components being presented without judgement.

Newtonian physics is the description and study of the objective, observ-
able matter's response to applied forces. Quantum physics and astrophysics
are needed to discuss the flow of material on imperceivably small and large
levels (Kerion, 2010). On these levels, the world functions in different ways.
The rules of this one, classically Newtonian level do not apply to the rules of
the archetypal. Analogously, the work of Jung was the movement from the
personal psyche and its psychology to the inclusion of archetypal and collective consciousness and their influence on the personal psyche. Individuation
is the movement from the personal levels of the psyche to the inclusion of
the collective levels of family, cultural, ancestral, archetypal, and the Self.
Therefore, the conscious reflection on synchronicities aids in awareness of
the occurring archetype. The more archetypal awareness gained by a perceiving consciousness, the further in the individuation path they have traveled.
This is how synchronicities guide the individuation process—that is, through
educative means.

JUNGIAN, ARCHETYPAL ASTROLOGY
OF PISCES TO AQUARIUS AIONS

Astrology is the use of the celestial bodies' orientations to reveal psychological, archetypal, and mythological connections (Le Grice, 2010). The
whole system is based on the utilization and recognition of synchronicity.
Astrologically, we are on the great Aion transition from Pisces to Aquarius.
In astrology, each Aion is represented by a zodiac figure. According to the
astrological calendar, the age of Pisces is ending, and the age of Aquarius
is beginning. The transition occurs between the years of 2000 and 2200,
depending on the start date. The two signs are symbols of the archetypes
governing the collective psyche during the roughly 2,150 years of each Aion
(Jung, 1951/1968).

Von Franz discusses the psychological experience of time in her book
Psyche and Matter (1992). She illustrates one model of time as a sphere with
concentric spheres (1992, p.122). The innermost sphere is the timeless archetypes or archetypal images of Self. These do not change. Moving outward,
the layer after that is the archetypes of Aions. These are the archetypal images
governing the era of each millennium (Von Franz, 1992). The archetypal
image that represents the governing archetype of each Aion can be called the
God or Goddess overseeing the era. Therefore, Jung's description of the two
signs is a description of the archetypes governing these Aions.

The causal skeptic may point out that each Aion is based on star clusters to which humans have attributed meaning and names. Therefore, humans have created meaning where there is not any. Even the mythological symbols of Pisces and Aquarius are the labels assigned by modern man. However, as Greene points out, Jung did not believe that symbols were social constructions (2018, p. 5). Jung saw symbols as having ontological status and that the symbols were discovered, not fabricated. Collective symbols, or symbols from whole traditions, were perceiving consciousness's way of interpreting archetypes. The synchronicity of other mythologies identifying the same types of changes during the apocalypse supports this archetypal astrological interpretation.

Of course, this great shift from Pisces to Aquarius starts with the ending of Pisces. Jung describes the Pisces Aion, the sign of two fish, as being governed by these two fish or two brothers at odds (Jung, 1951/1968). Jung thought Christ to be the first, vertical fish, and the inverse fish was the anti-Christ. This Aion was governed by two polar dualities, which defied resolution (Jung 1951/1968). The lack of resolution manifested as mass destruction psychologically, politically, and environmentally. The main feature of the Aion is this conflict of opposites. Jung said this division put a split in the hearts of people, which rips apart their psyche (1951/1968). Externally, this is reflected in the destruction of the natural environment and innumerable wars.

Jung said the transition from the two opposing forces into the unified being required the recognition of evil as an entity, not the just the absence of good (1951/1968). The recognition of evil can only be done by bringing it forth from the collective shadow and integrating it. When evil is recognized as an entity, then individuals' projections onto each other can be withdrawn and a transcendent position and perspective may emerge. It rises above the conflict and raises the combatants' interaction to a new, higher level. This allows the establishment of a "third," higher position that allows evolution to kick back into gear and proceed apace after the resolved conflict.

This third position is not given, however, which is the meaning of the Latin maxim *tertium non datur*. Like all educative acts, which at their profoundest level take discourse to a novel, higher plane of possibility, the interaction that was previously conflictual becomes, through the magic of dialectic, a new level of discourse. This dynamic is the essence of all truly educative processes.

The result is apperceptive stability, a harmony within the human psyche (Jung, 1951/1968). The rip within the collective psyche, mirrored within the individual, will be healed through this work. The divide is not simply within the psyche but within the false divides, such as with the psyche and the environment. Jung says the resolution of the conflict will have to occur on the individual level (1951/1968). Pisces was also the age of monotheistic and organized religions, where the collective systems tell individuals what to do. This is exemplified by the heavy influence that religion has had in the political sphere.

Both Aquarius and Pieces involve water, but Aquarius is the individual water bearer. This signifies the differences between the two signs in their relationship to the psyche, represented by water. In Pieces it had more to do with collective organization providing the means for the individual to relate to the Self. In the later period of Aquarius, the water carrier bears the water himself. This indicates the individual is more responsible for the relation to Self. These individuals having to resolve the collective conflicts within themselves signifies the beginning of Aquarius, the Aion of individual responsibility. The Aion is a collective educator of an entire epoch, helping it orient/discover itself in all sorts of ways.

The Aion of Aquarius, the water carrier, is the era of the individual carrying their own spirituality and collective responsibility (Greene, 2018). In other words, the change between Aions is from the collective to the individual as the focus. This is not to say that the Aion is one of solo individuals or individualism. Rather, the individual has a requirement for greater consciousness of the collective groups, archetypal psyche, and Self. The individual must take responsibility for their relationship to the greater whole, internally and externally. The fish swim within the water, but the sign here is the water carrier. Under the sign of Pisces, the individual is within the collective organization, both politically and religiously. Under the sign of Aquarius, the individual holds the water, representing spirituality, life force, and spirit. Given that water can also symbolize the psyche, this transition indicates a great shift in our understanding of the psyche as well. Moreover, the educational shift is from education for inclusion in the collective to education for Self-realization.

Herein lies a great paradox in the history of U.S. education. Whereas in the opening decades of the 20th century, left-leaning educationists called for curricula that equipped the student for collectivist purposes and saw knowledge as socially constructed (Counts, 1935; Dewey, 1916) liberal curriculum theorists today stress the uniqueness of the individual and the danger that collectivism and centralized government of any stripe poses to each person's epistemological sovereignty. This is but one example from education itself that mirrors this overarching dynamic in many areas of human endeavor. It is a subtle shift away from the social construction of knowledge for collective purposes and toward the cultivation of the individual's perspectives and purposes *qua* an individual. Giddens calls this the world-historical movement toward "the politics of self-identity" in the more developed countries (1991). Here as elsewhere, these two contiguous Aions disclose themselves in a particular discrete form as well as in their general field dynamics in their most crucial aspect: As cosmic educators for humanity. They are where the mind of the human being meets the mind of God (Jung, 1935/1976).This sometimes occurs in the individual in the revelatory form of him forging a new, reenergized personal narrative; other times it happens in the collective form of a new national narrative in which the citizens find new hope, renewed vision and higher aims; in this, they dwell within an elevated view that a nation has of itself (Mayes, 2020).

The two signs' description shows what is changing but does not depict the way or the means. This is what Le Grice said was a significant struggle of our time: the absences of mythology or trust in mythology to help guide the process (2010). Transitioning from one Aion to the next, constellating the archetype of death-rebirth or apocalypse, is neither simple nor pleasant. Jung saw this as a time of great turmoil (1951/1968). The turmoil adds to the destruction seen at the end of the Pisces era.

Coming to terms with evil and healing the fractured psyche is the individuation process. Facing the issue and entering into the complex creates great disruption to the ego. Furthermore, the resolution is not even guaranteed. This is so because deep conceptual change, which is the goal of all educative processes, is invested with our passionate commitments in all the most gripping aspects of our lives: the physical, cognitive, emotional, cultural, ethical, and spiritual. In what follows, I identify and discuss three themes common to all three myths: (1) large-scale destruction, (2) healing through the recognition and integration of evil, and (3) the primacy of the individual. In each section, I show the educative source and consequence of those three elements.

HOPI AND CHRISTIAN MYTHOLOGIES
AND THEIR VISIONARIES

Von Franz says that it is in looking back that one can clearly see the connection between synchronistic events (1992). Indeed, there is no way to scientifically predict when synchronistic events are going to occur. The oracular traditions, divinations, and visions from visionaries seemingly connect to the imperceptible archetypal patterns to make predictions regarding inner and outer occurrences. All three mythologies have visionaries and visionary experiences to light the way forward between the two eras. And whereas the scientific method demands replicability, the visionary is known by the revelatory and revolutionary uniqueness of his vision.

The Hopi are people whose traditions place the spiritual and ceremonial above all else. The Hopis' mythological descriptions of the past three worlds align with possible literal environmental changes. Their mythology attributes the environmental problems to the loss of the spiritual wellness of the people (Waters, 1963). The Hopi saw the external changes as manifestations of the imbalance of good and evil, or the spiritual state of the people. Their predictions of the transition from the fourth to the fifth world evolves out of this mythology. The Hopi have had three worlds end. Each ended with massive environmental disruption.

The first was by fire, the second by ice, and the third by water. The fourth is to end in war, political corruption, and mass extinction (Clements, 2004). Each time they left a world, they followed the stars and the mythic figures, who then guided them to their new home. Here, divinations and prophecies, such as those that are inherent in the entire astrological enterprise, serve the distinctly educative function of mystically apprising a people of its present condition and what its future course should or could be. In this sense, divinations and prophecies are a sort of transcendent curriculum for a people.

Joy Harjo is a Native American poet, who has recently become the first Native American poet laureate of the United States. In this volume is a particularly gripping poem called "Map to the Next World." The poem is symbolic instructions for traveling from the Fourth to the Fifth World, aligning with Hopi mythology (Harjo, 2001). This poem (Appendix A) was inspired by the synchronistic event of a multitude of butterflies heralding the birth of her granddaughter. The poem came from a synchronistic event and depicts not only the two worlds' governing archetypes but also the process necessary to make the transition. The poem starts with the description of this era's destruction (Harjo, 2001). This is in alignment with Jung's description of the end of Pisces. Harjo also describes the need for the journeyer to face the collective rages and monsters killing everyone (2001). This is her depiction of evil. The need to face it is another way of saying it must be recognized and integrated. Individuals are able to navigate to the Fifth World by discovering their own maps that can only be read by star light (Harjo, 2001). The process Harjo depicts with this imagery is the process of individuation. Synchronistically, this echoes Jung's observation that the work must be done individually in order to enter the era of Aquarius.

In Christianity, the final book of the New Testament is Revelations, John's vision of an apocalypse (2020). The book starts with the discussion of Christ and moves into John's vision of the apocalypse. The vision starts with massive destruction and disruption of the Earth. There is a confrontation with evil, represented by a dragon and Satan. The stars are then knocked out of the sky. A woman arises and gives birth to new baby, which the dragon tries to eat. The baby is kept safe by angels and heaven (Newman, 2010). John reassures the people by saying those who are living in the right way will hide until it is safe to emerge after the new beginnings have arrived. John's words are similar to Harjo's end of her poem. She says the Fifth World will begin when the last person has climbed the ladder within their heart out of the destruction (Harjo, 2001).

According to Greene, Jung was a visionary of archetypal astrology (2018). For further description of how to transition from the Pisces to Aquarius, Greene suggests looking at Jung's *Red Book* (2018). Greene says Jung's The *Red Book* thus offers itself as another synchronistic source of guidance for this archetypal shift. Jung was deeply aware of archetypal movements of the collective, as well as in his personal life. Besides his psychological development, his vast resources of knowledge from around the world and his travels connected his personal psyche to the collective unconscious, especially when world-historical shifts were in the mystical air. Jung wrote,

> A spiritual goal that points beyond the purely natural man and his worldly existence is an absolute necessity for the health of the soul; it is the Archimedean point from which alone it is possible to lift the world off its hinges and to transform the natural state into a cultural one. (Jung, 1946/1954, p. 86)

The connection between the prophetic enterprise and the pedagogical one is nowhere made clearer in Jung than here; he reminds us that the goal of both is cultural evolution into ways and means of social interaction that are more beautiful and humane. Here is the answer to Hobbes's grim notice in *Leviathan* that human existence is "nasty, brutish, and short." Rather, the pedagogical and prophetic cry to humanity is finally the same, as Lord Tennyson proclaimed at the end of his poem *Ulysses*: "Come, my friends. 'Tis not too late to seek a newer world."

THE SYNCHRONICITIES: HOW THE
THREE MYTHOLOGIES ALIGNED

As the reader has probably already noted, in this chapter the term "apocalypse" is in most instances understood symbolically as the death of the mythology governing an era or society. This is not a literal end of the world. The fact that each of these mythologies align indicates that they are channeling the same death-rebirth archetype. Maybe synchronistically our era is so intently focused on apocalyptic myths and stories that we are seeking guidance to help navigate through the death and rebirth of our current mythology because we are seeking some form of divine guidance in the face of our current mythology's demise.

I have attempted in this chapter to adumbrate that prophecy is transcendental pedagogy and pedagogy as the transcendence concretized in educative acts, as Jung following Haggle's dialectical views applied to education. Another point of connection between the three myths is their reliance on, and seeking guidance from, the stars. All these traditions invoke the stars as reflection of the impending changes of the world and collective psyche. Archetypal astrology uses the stars as an outer reflection of the psychic changes for individuals and the collective. In Christianity, the Christ child was heralded by the stars. The story tells of the three wiseman arriving to welcome the birth of the child. The birth of the Christ was the beginning of the preceding Aion. It may have been possible that the wisemen were also paying attention to the synchronicities of their time.

In *Revelations*, the dragon, or Satan, knocks the stars from the sky. The stars represent the angelic forces of good and guidance (Newman, 2010). In the Hopi mythology, the people find their way to their home in the next world guided by the stars. During some of these transitions between worlds, only the people living in harmony and connection to the Creator can see the guiding stars (Waters, 1963).

While there are other apocalyptic prophecies that align with this current era and events, the three discussed here are some of the most documented and most studied. Besides the theme of the stars and the prediction of a world's end, each mythology shares three common themes. First, each myth predicts mass destruction socially and politically. Second, the mythologies say the individuals living in "proper ways" will live on and are needed to start the next era. Third is the recognition of evil, which when faced leads to peace, prosperity, and healing in relationship to the natural world and concomitantly to the empowerment of the archetypal feminine.

The recurrence of the same major themes strongly suggests the presence of synchronicity. Each of the prophesies was created in a different part of world, at different times, without knowledge of each other. Permeating myths and prophecies from all times and places, and embedded in prophecies and myths everywhere and always, synchronicity is the master teacher in the "universal schoolhouse" of the cosmos (Moffett, 1994).

DESTRUCTION

The appearance of synchronicities can be disruptive, like the trickster shaking the ego to make room for something new (Combs & Holland, 1996). All three prophecies involve disaster. Looking at disaster as a trickster shaking the ego, the destruction signifies the death needed to make space for the rebirth. *Revelations'* prophesy focuses mostly on destruction (King James Bible, 2020). John sees seven seals on scrolls. As each is broken, he sees the related ensuing destruction. There are the four horsemen of the apocalypse: war, famine, pestilence, and death. The sixth seal opens earthquakes, the blackening of the sun, the loss of mountains and islands. The people must hide (Newman,

2010). The Hopi's mythology describes the Fourth world's end as a time of extinction, war, and corruption (Clements, 2004).

Similarly, death and resurrection are the archetypal pattern that must more or less prevail in educative spaces where the prophetic function prevails. But why death? What place does it have in any enlightened and humane teaching and learning situation? The inexpugnability of all in the irony of this is captured by the student's experience of intellectual death (what the Zen teacher in Herrigel's *Zen and the Art of Archery* called "shipwreck") does the student find new intellectual, moral, and spiritual life (1971). Indeed, one might say that the instructional cycle of spiritual classroom is defined by the Passion and the Resurrection: It leads from the Cross, on which our old conceptions must be nailed, to the Risen Lord of our consciousness in the spirit finding new transcendent view. The effects of such balanced instruction on the student are quick, dramatic, and durable. Said Yogananda in his autobiography, *The Autobiography of a Yogi,*

> I am immeasurably grateful for the humbling blows [Sri Yukteswar, Yogananda's teacher and guru] dealt my vanity. I sometimes feel that, metaphorically, he was discovering and uprooting every diseased tooth in my jaw. The hard core of egotism is difficult to dislodge except rudely. With its departure, the Divine finds at last an unobstructed channel. In vain it seeks to percolate through flinty hearts of selfishness. (Yogananda, 1946, p. 141)

Indeed, as noted above, conceptual change theory informs us that a change in thinking is rarely a matter of simply weighing evidence, pro and con, and then coming to an impersonal assessment of a discursive claim or actual situation. Rather, what counts as evidence of something, how it is processed through the schemata are the guidance system of our lives in the world of consensual reality, and how we choose to either put or not put our conclusions into action is an incalculably complex matter. It involves the whole person, her complete life-narrative with all of its commitments at the personal, familial, cultural, and ethical constructs that are not just crucial elements in her life. They *are* her life.

It is no small thing to give up one worldview, even in part, and take on another. It can be a kind of emotional and ideological death for the student. But this is the hallmark of the prophetic announcement. As that most prophetic of poets, Rainer Maria Rilke declared, "Du musst dein Leben ändern!" "You must change your life!" (2001).

In a universe where the only constant is creative evolution, pedagogy and prophecy have this in common: They are calling out, like John the Baptist in the wilderness, for us to put off the old garments of an otiose tradition (but keeping and honoring what was true and beautiful in that tradition) and putting on the new attire of new era. Prophecy that serves no communal purpose is mere ranting in the wind; pedagogy that serves no transcendental purpose inevitably devolves into a profane pedagogy in which the teacher is both threatened and coerced into becoming merely a creature of the state. However, when prophecy and pedagogy so blend into each other in the service of humankind's single greatest project—our evolution in and toward the divine—then will we proclaim, individuals but in unison, that

> We shall not cease from exploration
> And the end of all our exploring
> Will be to arrive where we started
> And know the place for the first time.
> Through the unknown, unremembered gate
> When the last of earth left to discover
> Is that which was the beginning.

(Eliot, 1971)

By examining the three myths at their archetypal core we have seen that, despite surface differences, they make similar predictions about the end of the world. Importantly, however, these predictions are not to be taken literally but as psycho spiritual events in the cultural unconscious. As such they serve an educative function in a culture, in that if it heeds these prophesies, it will not only survive but prevail. If it does not, it is destined to fail and ultimately fall. Thus, as in the great Protestant essentialist theologian Paul Tillich, the scriptural reference to the separation from the children of light and the child of darkness is primarily an individual phenomena as light and dark elements are separated and dealt with by that individual, or not. In other words, in Jung's terms the individual does or does not do their shadow work. Those who do experience the redemptive state of individuation as the successful operation of the transcendent function. The myth is therefore educatively instructive at both the macro-cultural and micro-individual levels.

REFERENCES

Cambray, J. (2009). *Synchronicity: Nature and psyche in the interconnected universe.* Texas A&M University Press.

Clements, W. (2004). "A continual beginning, and then an ending, and then a beginning again": Hopi Apocalypticism in the New Age. *Journal of the Southwest, 46*(4), 643–60. Retrieved from https://www.jstor.org/stable/40170280

Counts, G. (1935). *Dare the schools build a new social order* (pamphlet). Nation Education Association.

Combs, A., & Holland, M. (1996). *Synchronicity: Through the eyes of science, myth, and the trickster*. Marlowe & Company.

Dewey, J. (1916). *Democracy and education*. Free Press.

Eliot, T. S. (1971). *Complete poems and plays of T. S. Eliot: 1909 to 1950*. Harcourt, Brace and World Inc.

Greene, L. (2018). *The astrological world of Jung's Liber Novus: Daimons, gods, and the planetary journey*. Routledge.

Harjo, J. (2001). *A map to the next world: Poetry and tales*. W.W. Norton & Norton.

Herrigel, E. (1971). *Zen and the art of archery.* Vintage Book

Hillman, J. (2007). *Mythic figures*. Spring Publications.

Hobbes, T. (1651/2010). *Leviathan: Or the matter, forme, and power of a common-wealth ecclesiasticall and civill*, ed. by Ian Shapiro (Yale University Press; 2010).

Huebner, D. (1999). *The lure of the transcendent: Collected essays by Dwayne E. Huebner*, ed. V. Hillis. Lawrence Erlbaum Associates, 1999.

Jung, C. G. (1954). Analytical psychology and education (R. F. C. Hull, Trans.). In H. Read et al. (Eds.), *The collected works of C. G. Jung: Vol. 17. Development of personality* (pp. 63–132). Princeton University Press. (Original work published 1946)

Jung, C.G. (1960). *Synchronicity: An acausal connecting principle*. Princeton University Press.

Jung, C. G. (1968). *Aion: Researches into the phenomenology of the self* (R. F. C. Hull, Trans.) (H. Read et al., Eds.), *The collected works of C. G. Jung* (Vol. 09ii, 2nd ed. pp. 72–94). Princeton University Press. (Original work published 1951).

Jung, C. G. (1976). XII psychology and religion (R. F. C. Hull, Trans.). In H. Read et al. (Eds.), *The collected works of C. G. Jung: Vol. 18. The symbolic life* (pp. 663–70). Princeton University Press. (Original work published 1935).

Jung, C.G. (2009). *The red book: Liber Novous (A reader's edition)*. Shamdasani, S. (Ed.). W.W. Norton & Company.

King James Bible Online. (2020). *Revelations. King James Bible Online*. https://www.kingjamesbibleonline.org/Revelation-Chapter-1/

Le Grice, K. (2010). *The archetypal cosmos: Rediscovering the gods in myth, science and astrology*. Edinburgh, Scotland: Floris Books.

Mayes, C. (2020). *Archetype culture and the individual: The three pedagogical narratives*. Routledge.

Giddens, A. (1991). *Modernity and self identity*. Palo Alto: Stanford University Press.

Moffett, J. (1994). *Universal schoolhouse: Spiritual awakening through education*. Jossey-Bass.

Newman, S. (2010). *The real history of the end of the world*. Berkley Books.

Rilke, R. (2001). *The torso of apollo*. Schocken Press.

Skinner, B. F. (1968). *The technology of teaching.* Prentice Hall.

Tennyson, A. (2013). *Alfred, Lord Tennyson: An anthology*. Cambridge University Press.

Von Franz, M. L. (1992). *Psyche and matter*. Shambhala.

Waters, F. (1963). *Book of the Hopi*. Penguin Books.

Yogananda (1946). *The autobiography of the yogi*. The Self-Realization Followship.

Chapter 7

Creative Evolution in the Pedagogical Moment

Kevin A. Kell

"The master is not someone with nothing left to learn. The master is merely the best student."

—Kevin Red Bear Dubrow (personal communication, 2010)

The sentiment articulated in this quote is certainly not unique to Red Bear. However, he lived in accord with this sentiment throughout his life, constantly seeking out new learning, books, and teachers. After a lifetime of study, the books and authors he regarded as foundational to a life well-lived stand out as especially significant. Perhaps it is no wonder that one such author he recommended at almost every workshop was one he himself spent a lifetime reading and studying, Joseph Campbell.

In my model of teaching and learning, Joseph Campbell's work on the Hero archetype is particularly relevant. In *The Hero with a Thousand Faces* (1949), Campbell divided his book into two sections. The first section covers the material that most are familiar with, which is often called the "the Hero's Journey" even though Campbell called it the "monomyth" (1949, p. 1). This first part, exploring the archetypal stages of the hero's quest, is some of his most cited work and has been referred to in the creation of works with profound cultural significance such as the Star Wars movies as well as others.

The second half of *Hero with a Thousand Faces* puts that Hero's journey into a greater cosmic context. Critics of Campbell and the hero archetype decry this journey as being one of masculine conquest and the triumph of the ego. However, a more accurate study of Campbell's work reveals instead that the monomyth is not about conquest but about initiation, often through defeat

(1949). As Campbell stated, "Where we had thought to slay another, we shall slay ourselves. . . . And where we had thought to be alone, we will be with all the world" (1949, p. 18). This journey is not about ego inflation but about individuation, the process described by C. G. Jung as the realization of the potentials of the individual (Jung, 1950/1969). And additionally in this quote, it is clear too that this process is not one of individuation into isolation, but a process that finds the individual *more* imbedded in the interdependence of the universe.

A person in the individuation process does not feel it to be glorious at the time, for as Jung wrote about individuation, "*the experience of the self is always a defeat for the ego*" (Jung, 1955–56/ 1970, p. 546, italics in original). It is through this defeat, however, that the questor is able to deepen, learn, and transform in order to return to the people with a boon. This boon renews not only the hero themselves but the community as well. Campbell contextualized this process as a continuous unfolding and transformation of the cosmos (1949). The hero's journey is a continuation of the creation of the universe in the same way that Alan Watts discussed the Big Bang as not being a discrete event of the long past but a never-ending process that is embodied by each of us in the unfolding of our lives (Watts, 1989).

The hero in this sense is a perpetual learner personally but also in a transpersonal sense. The learning of the hero is not an inflation of the drive to power and certainly is not reduceable to a sublimation of sexual libido. This learning is a cosmic act of creation and a fundamental aspect of the individuation journey. Understood in this sense, individuation is therefore a collective act as well as a deeply personal one. When a person individuates, it is also the individuation of the *anima mundi*, the soul of the world, to some extent as well.

To illustrate this point, Watts uses another image: when one looks at flowers in a field, one might say that the field is flowering, not just the individual plant is flowering (Watts, 1989). This perspective recognizes that without the field, the flowers could not appear and that they are appearing out of a larger process interdependent with their surrounding eco system. Or, as the Renaissance English poet the Reverend John Donne wrote, "No man is an island, entire of itself; every man is a piece of the continent, a part of the main." (Donne, 1624/1959, p. 109)

In this same way, a person's individuation process is to some extent dependent on the context and collective processes around them. Thus, when the hero returns with the boon at the end of the quest, as is described in Campbell's work, this boon is the result not just of an individual process, but the collective process manifesting within the individual. This boon is not solely a renewal for the individual but is the very process by which the collective is renewed as well.

In the previous volume of this series (Kell, 2021a), I discussed how the archetypes of teacher and learner are experienced as inherently meaningful, in a vocational sense. This interpenetration of the personal and collective evolutionary processes offers a possible ontological explanation for why this might be the case.

This idea of cosmological development is also discussed theologically within creative evolution (Bergson, 1965/1902). Within this theological perspective, the divine is not the "unmoved Mover" of Aristotle's *Metaphysics*. Instead, the divine is itself constantly evolving (Bergson, 1965/1902). Thus, the human psyche is not an isolated point in the universe. The human psyche is like a wave in the ocean of the ever emerging and developing cosmic ocean.

To be a teacher then is not separate from this sacred journey but an intrinsic outgrowth and development of it (Mayes, 2005). Not only must one first be a student in order to have anything worth teaching but also being a teacher at a certain point constitutes an essential continuation of one's cosmic studentry. And yet, it is not enough to be an unconscious student or teacher. Beginning to teach requires that one also develop some working conscious understanding of this process: how best to facilitate it in others as well as how this sacred duty also functions within one's own process of individuation.

Jung wrote that one "can hardly draw a veil over the fact that we psychotherapists ought really to be philosophers or philosophical doctors—or rather that we already are so" (Jung, 1946/1966, *CW 16*, para. 181). The same can be said of teachers. It is essential that teaching be constructed and informed by a robust practice model and pedagogical theory that guides specific concrete directions, one that is holarchically understood within the larger cosmological context.

Mayes offers one way of picturing a holarchy:

> a system of circles nested within circles—all on one plane, no circle "above" another one. This is the emergence of ever broader circles radiating out of circles, all emanating concentrically as if from a point in the pond where a stone was initially dropped in an act of creation. This is to indicate that each circle, each "domain," is essential to the functioning of the entire system . . . and thus no domain is more important than the other. Rupture one of the rings in the circle and the entire system breaks down. Yet the circles *are* concentric, indicating that each circle is more complex than the ones from which it emanated. (Mayes, 2019, p. 29)

This model thus meets the modern political imperative that a democratic political and even ontological economy be egalitarian but also that different levels of complexity also be acknowledged. Thus, there is differentiation but without hegemony in a holarchy.

In practical terms, this requires that common misconceptions of teaching and obstacles be worked through in order for this process to be successful individually and interpersonally.

Teaching is of course not limited to what is sometimes called the "traditional classroom." This is one place where teaching and learning take place but teaching and learning are processes that can be constellated in countless settings. Therefore, the discussion here is intended to address teaching and learning wherever they take place. Anytime teaching and learning are happening, I refer to that as a constellation of the pedagogical moment. In this way, anyone regardless of their profession can develop applications of the current discussion whether in the raising of children, the mentoring of colleagues, or the informing of customers.

Because the processes of teaching and learning are essential to the process of individuation, it is beneficial to think of the field of archetypal pedagogy not as limited to a classroom setting but as pertinent to any constellations of the pedagogical moment. A more accurate title for the field has been discussed as "archetypal pedagogics" to reflect this more general application (Mayes, personal communication, 2018).

Teaching is a sacred duty. Teaching is not the aggrandizement of the teacher through an inflation of knowing that fuels a one-up-one-down power trip. Those with things worth sharing have a responsibility to teach. Our learning is not our own or our possession to horde. As social creatures, learning and teaching are at the heart of what makes us human. Novelist Philip Pullman thus has one of his characters say that "for a human being, nothing comes naturally[;] . . . we have to learn everything we do" (Pullman, 1997/ 2007, p. 515).

In *The Sibling Society* (1977), Robert Bly discussed the idea that in an evolutionary exchange for our brain size, we evolved to be born unfinished as a species. What we lose in instinctual knowing and reflexive abilities, we more than make up for with plastic capacity for learning (Bly, 1977). This leads to our astonishing adaptability as a species. Since humans are born "unfinished," they must then be taught to become successful members of their community. This learning forms what we refer to as culture, that is, the cultivation of human beings.

The cultivation of human beings is both an art form and a technology that has developed since our species began to emerge. Culture is an information-based technology in that it is an application of knowledge and wisdom to achieve and improve a goal. Simultaneously, culture is an art form because there are innumerable creative decisions to be made based on values, aesthetics, and various fiduciary commitments. Any one culture, and culture in general, is refined by each generation for subsequent generations to benefit from, add to, and adapt to current need.

What we learn from others and even the framing of our own experiences is the latest episode in the interconnected web of human learning. In *A Hitchhiker's Guide to the Galaxy*, Adams wrote that the Earth was created as a giant computer meant to produce the ultimate question about life, the universe, and everything (Adams, 2005). Fittingly, the Earth was subsequently destroyed to make way for an intergalactic super-highway right as the final question was discovered.

This image provides a viable metaphor for the interconnected nature of our "individual" learning processes. Each human psyche is like a neuron in the collective, computer-like brain of humanity. In this way, our learning is never truly our own exclusively. And in this way, we have a responsibility to work through the questions before us, to the best of our ability, and pass on our answers and our work, however partial or incomplete they may be.

Being a learner and a teacher is thus one of the most intimately individual processes that we participate in and paradoxically also a transcendent, transpersonal, impersonal collective process as well. To mistake one's learning and discovery as ultimate would therefore constitute a *hubris* or inflation. The "Truth," with a capital "T," the ontological absolute, is at closest an asymptote: a line that can be approached ever closer but never be reached. Attuning ourselves to this Truth is also like dressing for the weather. We can dress appropriately but then we have to dress differently perhaps for tomorrow. The target is ever moving and ever receding beyond permanent reach. Learning and teaching in this archetypal sense amounts to a quest to reach this asymptote or spend a lifetime approaching ever closer.

ARCHETYPAL DANGERS

In *Power in the Helping Professions*, Adolf Guggenbühl-Craig discussed the danger of identifying conterminously with the Healer/Helper archetype (1971). He highlighted that within the helper-helped relationship, each must own both poles of the archetype: wounded and healer. If the healer refuses to own and integrate her own woundedness, then the client or patient is left with only the woundedness. The client then fails to constellate the healing archetype within, which is what does the healing in the first place. The same inflationary pitfall awaits the one who would over identify with the teacher archetype and forget her own nature as a learner.

In Jungian psychology, it is desirable and even unavoidable to participate in the archetype, but to identify with the archetype is to court disaster. A metaphor I use to illustrate this point in sessions with clients is electricity. The archetypal is the electricity going through the powerlines of the collective unconscious. When everything is working well, the electricity is transformed into a manageable intensity and channeled into our homes for use. This corresponds to participating in the archetype, and when we do, it powers our lives. To identify with the archetype would amount to climbing the power line poles and grabbing the terminals of the transformers directly. It is too much power for the psyche to hold individually.

One is able to participate in the teaching archetype without identifying with it by maintaining an awareness and practice of the truth, that the teacher is first and foremost a student themselves. This manifests in the continuation and development of one's knowledge base and in that each encounter with a student is an opportunity for continued learning as well. This allows the student to recognize that he is also always a teacher of himself and others.

Master psychotherapist and teacher Kevin Red Bear Dubrow would often tell a story at the beginning of certain workshops about the importance of asking questions. Earlier in his career, he was hired to deliver a program to an auditorium of students within a particular program for gifted students. At one point in the program, which were always interactional and dialogical, he read a poem he wrote that repeated the Ojibwe word for gratitude, "Miigwech."

After the poem, there was some discussion of it and yet not one person asked what this word meant. When Red Bear had clarified that they indeed did not know, he asked why no one was curious enough to ask him what it meant. A young lady in the front row raised her hand and answered, "We've been taught that if there's something that we need to know you [the teacher] will tell us." Much of the rest of the workshop was spent addressing this form of "training," how problematic it is, and how it should never be confused with "educating," which is responsible, dynamic, and creative. "Training" exists in the service of the technical maintenance of a given system. It thus by definition is antithetical to creative evolution, which is the very essence of true education.

The curiosity and initiative of these students were trained out of them, as is, unfortunately, the case with many students in the U.S. education system. This outcome persists despite years of focus on critical thinking skills. Education, reading, and even learning itself are experienced as burdens and requirements instead of the privilege, joy, and opportunity they are. This happens on systematic levels despite the best efforts of many individual teachers, administrators, and even individual schools within the larger societal system.

QUESTIONS

As an individual with ENFP preferences (Myers-Briggs Extroverted, Intuitive, Feeling, and Perceiving personality type), I love the dialogical learning of questions. Not only is this true for myself as a learner, but even more so when I teach. When presenting at conferences, the Q & A sessions after the talk are by far the most interesting and engaging part of the process for me. As a learning teacher, I find that through the questions of others, I am able to explore the topic from perspectives and in light of considerations that I had not thought of before. However enjoyable questions are for me as a teacher, they are also indispensable as a learner. A question reflects where a person is at in their process and conceptualization.

In this way, questions are highly useful diagnostically for a teacher. Yet too, the act of forming a question requires a cognitive consolidation and a *telos* move in the direction of learning. To deny students the opportunity for questions can therefore be detrimental to their learning selves and the pragmatic outcomes of learning. In some spiritual traditions, the teachers only ever answer questions because the questions show what the student is and is not ready to hear.

It is important to recognize that there are other methods of learning that are based on quiet observation and less on direct questioning, such as some within certain First Nation cultures. Yet, here, the essence is still that the learner is taking initiative with his or her observations and is taking responsibility for his or her own learning in the same way that I am suggesting with questions in other contexts. Even so, certain things are exceedingly difficult to simply glean from unnarrated observations. The essence is the taking of responsibility, and in some contexts, questions are one of the best ways to accomplish this effectively.

EPISTEMOLOGICAL CONSIDERATIONS
OF QUESTIONING

In his work with mentorees, Red Bear insisted on questioning as a fundamental aspect of the learning process (personal communication, 2009). He would say, "Question everything I say until it makes complete sense to you" (personal communication, 2009). For Red Bear, questioning was both a pedagogical necessity and fundamental to an empowered epistemology. Pragmatically, in the absence of questioning and rigorous exploration, there is a much greater risk of misunderstanding what is being communicated. Questioning reveals to the teacher the thought processes of the student and on what levels the student is engaging in the material. Through such a dialogic and questioning process, it is much more likely that misunderstandings can be identified and reconciled.

Within a process of individuation, questioning is also an essential basis for an empowerment epistemology. The symbols, images, information, models, and perspectives of one's teachers and traditions cannot be truly integrated without thorough dialogic engagement. In the absence of such depth-of-processing, the learning gained is at best a facsimile of real learning. Questioning facilitates a process whereby the student can explore the material as it relates to other experiences and previous interpretations. A learning process without questioning is additionally vulnerable to being coopted by projection and power dynamics, thwarting not only learning, but the student's own personal authority as well. Such arrangements are additionally racked with doubt, and worse, can lead to zealous, blind adherence to partial understandings and the prejudices that accompany them.

Questioning is epistemologically essential when the information one is gaining is novel, but it is especially important when the information one is receiving would challenge things that were previously held to be true. There are cases when one hears information that fits one's current conception of the world and simply adds to that existing content. While this information also needs to be scrutinized, it is the instances where there is contradictory information, which must be accommodated in a Piagetian sense, that one must not avoid rigorous questioning. It is in such moments that to avoid questioning would be most likely to lead to dangerous inflations or deflations.

Returning to Piaget's model for the development of any one schema, he theorized that when an individual encounters experiences that add information within the bounds of the current schema, this information is assimilated (Piaget, 1969). However, when experiences are encountered that challenge the schema framework itself, the schema must be changed to accommodate this new experience. In these terms, when something is encountered that challenges one's paradigm, one must question to facilitate the process of accommodating the new experiences and develop a new paradigm, or schema, that transcends but includes the previous one.

The implications and recommendations of such an epistemology are very consonant with the works of John Dewey and his models of education (1934, 1990). The emphasis is on self-discovery, even if it is withing contexts constructed carefully by teachers to facilitate the discovery. It is not a rejection of guidance but an emphasis on immanent, direct experience as a potent and robust epistemology of learning.

In the context of the metaphor of the asymptotic Truth, it is through this process of rupture, questioning, and new understanding that constitutes the progress toward the ever-receding line. All knowledge in this way is to some degree provisional, not in that it is wrong, but rather in that it is ultimately incomplete. Every person operates to some degree under illusions, things that are simply inaccurate or untrue. To suggest otherwise would be to transgress the teaching of the Buddha when he admonishes to remember that the biggest illusion is the notion that we have no illusions. Even so, understanding that is not illusory progresses similarly to the growth of a tree. While the tree grows, it does not change the previous arrangement of its branches, it elaborates and develops them further. The tree grows by becoming more of what it is, not by making itself something other.

Integrity as learner and teacher requires that one works to continually question new and existing paradigmatic material until clarity is found. Such clarity carries one forward until that clarity is again shaken and requires yet further questioning. Much anxiety and exploitation can be avoided by making this epistemological shift.

TEACHING AND EMPOWERMENT

In my work with clients, especially teens, I make sure to discuss this issue of belief and questioning in the first few sessions. I do not always lay out the full scope of the idea, but I at least introduce the essence. It is important because it helps establish the norm in the first session that I am not an unquestionable expert, the only agency in the room, leaving them as the object of my action. To be clear, there is a craft and knowledge base to therapy certainly, it is not all just a flaccid parody of Carl Rogers's "And how does that make you feel?"

However, assuming the mantle of the almighty-one creates a power differential that is not only distasteful but existentially untrue. My job is not to have all the answers. It is to facilitate a quality therapeutic process. In my model, while I can be very directive and psychoeducational, the intent is always to help clients find the empowerment to better understand themselves, the psyche, and to some degree the world. While I seek to share many fish, so to speak, my main intent is to teach them to fish as soon as possible. Far from creating an inflationary dependency on me, my job is to make myself redundant or otherwise teach and heal my way out of a job. What this introduces into the dynamic is an emphasis on empowerment over power.

I have written elsewhere some of my reflections on the inescapable nature of power and that it is not inherently toxic or corrupting as many would have one believe (Kell, 2021b). Power is a many-faceted thing with extensive written discussion from war and politics (Tzu, 2003), to personal efficacy (Greene, 2000), activism (Alinsky, 1971), and many others (Hillman, 1995). In my use of the term here, I am referring to the fact that constellating dynamics of power over and domination at the expense of the client's own subject and agency fails to develop the therapeutic relationship. Such power dynamics might even contribute to further trauma.

Power itself is essential for healthy living. We need to recognize what is and is not within our power and act responsibly with it. What becomes problematic is using that power to exploit others. In the teaching or therapeutic setting, there is a particular type of power that needs to be carefully attended to. This is the projective power that one gives another when the other person has something one wants.

Existentially, no one has power over us unless we give it to them by wanting something they have. Viktor Frankl discussed the contrapositive of this statement when he talked about freedom (2017, 1973). For Frankl, "man [is] a being whose main concern consists in fulfilling a meaning, rather than in the mere gratification of drives . . . or in mere adaptation and adjustment to society and environment" (2017, pp. 125–126). He wrote that, "life proves to be basically meaningful even when it is neither fruitful in creation nor rich in experience" because of "the person's attitude toward an unalterable fate" (1973, p. 44). He concluded that "a man's life retains its meaning up to the last—until he draws his last breath . . . [because] no matter how sparse the possibilities for realizing values may be—he has always the recourse to attitudinal values" (1973, pp. 44–45). I typically paraphrase this notion for clients by saying that we do not have the power to control our circumstances, but we always have the freedom to choose how we respond to those circumstances.

This is the essence of empowerment as I use the term. Empowerment is recognizing the truth that no one can impose their power and control over our ability to choose our response and having the audacity to choose responses that are meaningful, soul and life affirming, full of integrity, and dignity. In truth, this is something that no one can take away. However, American culture is so dominated by conditioning based on extrinsic motivation (Kohn) that by the time even middle-school age clients make it to my office, they are often either profoundly defeated or defiant. An important part of treatment is helping them to realize the empowerment they already possess and developing the courage to live from it.

While I cannot take power from someone that has not already projected it, there is still the moral imperative and responsibility to recognize that my position, role, not to mention gender, race, and physicality give me a power projection and privilege that must be handled ethically. And as Guggenbühl-Craig wrote, the degree to which this power is projected by the client is the degree to which they depotentiate themselves (1971).

I therefore seek to appropriately minimize the role that such power plays within the dynamic. I will retain enough power to ethically conduct my job and maintain the integrity of the office and process. Beyond that, it is incumbent upon me to help facilitate a process of retrieval of excess power projections by the client.

It bears mentioning that some amount of power projection is not only inescapable but necessary for the client's healing and development (Johnson, 2017). On one hand, they need to have some trust and faith in the process to even stick around and hear what I have to say, which requires some esteem for or confidence in me on their part. If I appear depotentiatiated with nothing to offer, most clients would not stay long enough to get help anyway, which would be irresponsible on my part.

Additionally, within multiple models it is beneficial for clients to see me with some sort of idealized projection. When doing object relations work, this helps provide certain object needs. For attachment theory work, this facilitates enough transference for me to provide a corrective emotional experience. For a depth psychological model, it helps me hold the client's projected gold (Johnson, 2017) to then help them learn to retrieve and own those qualities and characteristics. In a developmental or even skill-building sense, such projections also constitute a Vygotskian scaffolding and thereby facilitates the healing and growth process.

While these reflections are largely based on my clinical work as a therapist, these features are also prominent in my work as a consultant, a tutor, a supervisor, and the myriad other teaching-based roles I fill. In this way, being a teacher transcends the transaction of knowledge transfer and technical training.

This also touches on how the three archetypes of vocation I discussed in the first volume of this series (Kell, 2021a)—teacher, healer, and artist—are not discrete and distinct from one another but are in fact fractally nested within each other *ad infinitum*. It is in part by holding these projections and facilitating these processes conscientiously that one in a teacher role is also constellating and embodying the archetype of healer as well.

Requiring that a student or client believe me instead of question me reinforces a very skewed and problematic power dynamic, the presence of which in her life in other relationships may have contributed to why she came to therapy in the first place. What I would essentially be asking or requiring the client to do is to disregard their own process, their own experience, and any number of internal loci of control in favor of bestowing that power and authority on to me. Even if this process is "successful" and they adopt unquestioningly my experiences and conclusions, I have so undermined their own autonomy as to self-defeatingly sabotage the basis of the healing and learning process entirely.

This clinical principle is similar to the educational conclusion that Freire (1968) came to in *Pedagogy of the Oppressed*. There he discovered that a curriculum conforming to a set program of liberation (in his case a Marxist one) may liberate the student from an old oppressor but that it also now makes them subject to an ideology that was imposed on them without their consent by a teacher who now, as the representative of that ideology, becomes himself the new oppressor.

Such a process also carries with it an inescapably greater likelihood for misunderstanding and miscommunication. With no questions or dialogue to reflect back how the student is understanding what is presented, there is no way to gain one's bearings as a teacher as to what is and is not being understood. Continuing to subsequent topics with only the illusion of initial understanding has the potential for numerous complications. In contrast, promoting a process of trust and faith, and questioning ensures or at least inclines the client toward a model of ownership, intrinsic motivation, and empowered understanding.

TEACHER'S EMPOWERMENT

Of course, it bears discussing the teacher's relationship to and capacity for empowerment. Rarely if ever is one able to provide something to another that they do not have already for themselves. In this case, it would be almost impossible for a teacher to facilitate the development of the students' empowerment without first having a solid grounding in her own. In many helping traditions, before one becomes the helper, they must have first gone through their own process of being helped. When this fails to happen, it usually results in problematic dynamics and substandard process and outcomes.

In this case, without a grounding in a foundation of empowerment, the teacher will have nothing else to fall back on than the sabotaging dynamics of power. It is therefore necessary for the would-be teacher to sufficiently work through whatever issues are undermining or threaten to undermine his authority. As discussed before, power predominates when an individual wants something from another.

For the helper, there are many potential pitfalls in this arena that must be avoided. Other than a baseline of decency and safety, and respectfulness, a therapist or teacher should ideally want nothing from the student or client except fulfilling the terms of the contract, such as payment. Any desires beyond this should be immediately inspected for issues of codependence and counter transference. One operationalization of this principle is that a therapist should not want the client to get better more than the client does. Failing to accommodate this principle thwarts the healing process by having the therapist chase the client or otherwise attempt to drag the client into health. In any case, it undermines the client's work and development with undue pressure.

Some other common traps that therapists and to some degree teachers can fall into include wanting admiration, wanting respect, wanting to be liked, wanting to be loved, wanting to be treated as an expert, wanting to belong, wanting approval, wanting favorable outcomes, and wanting the student or client to stay in the helping process forever, if not at least only terminating on the terms of the therapist. Wanting to be liked, loved, respected, or otherwise approved of are challenges faced by many clinicians and teachers especially at the beginning their career.

The fantasy of helping grateful clients and students that return all investments of care with effort and esteem is indeed a seductive one. However, whether such dynamics are likely or not, to the degree that a therapist *needs* these things from the client is the degree to which the client has power over the therapist and by extension has coopted and corrupted the therapeutic process.

The therapeutic process does not require the therapist to have power over the client. As discussed above, such a dynamic is fraught and often problematic. However, it is also true that successfully therapy cannot take place if the client is given power over the therapist. While my practice model is deeply client centered and even client led where indicated, even such client-directed models are threatened if the therapist is not able to maintain the integrity of the process through their own empowerment.

I have seen directly and second hand how these otherwise benign-appearing entanglements derail the therapy process in subtle ways that can have escalating consequences. To be clear, most everyone enjoys being liked. The question at hand is whether this desire is allowed to influence one's actions and decision and thereby compromise the process.

Another insidious way that power dynamics slink into the otherwise noble intentions of helping professionals is in the need for clients to get better. In teaching terms, it would be the need for students to learn. Red Bear used to summarize this concern by admonishing that the therapist should never want a client to get better more than the client wants to get better (personal communication). What Red Bear summarized succinctly can be found discussed in greater depth in books such as *Power in the Helping Professions* (1971) by Guggenbühl-Craig and *Back to One* (1977), by Sheldon Kopp. The need to have the clients get better, or the student learn, puts the responsibility onto the therapist and teacher in a way that gives clients' issues and students' ignorance power over the would-be helper.

This undermines the real outcomes and is also one of the most common reasons for burnout in the helping professions. Guggenbühl-Craig's discussion showed how this arrangement deflates the helped and inflates the helper (1971). This furthermore usually leads to passivity on the part of the helped and anxiety on the part of helper. In *Back to One,* Kopp recommended that to address this issue, the therapist needs to remain vigilantly aware instead of what he *is* responsible for: providing impeccable therapeutic service (1977). Essentially, it is not then up to the therapist what the client does or does not do with this provision.

It would be possible to misperceive this posture as an abdication of one's responsibilities to the client. However, it is important to remember the cliché about leading a horse to water. In short, the therapist provides the water and then does what is possible to facilitate the horse drinking. Anything more would amount to waterboarding the horse.

In practical terms, it is essential to remember that "quality therapeutic services" inherently involves dialogic process of reflection, reassessment, and adjustments based on meeting the client where he or she is at. The key here is to recognize that the therapist is responsible for therapy, not the life and choices of the client.

In teaching terms, the above discussion would apply to any positive outcomes for learning, growth, or development that the teacher might hold for the student. Obviously, the point of teaching is to help facilitate learning, but there is a limit where the teacher has to accept that the students must choose to be active participants in their own learning and are not passive receptacles for the teacher to fill. Accepting these boundaries and limitations forms a substantial part of the empowerment of the teacher or therapist.

CONCLUSION

Thus, it is through the processes of active questioning and authentic self-exploration that students in any pedagogical moment are able to constellate the learner/teacher archetypes and thus continue their process of individuation. Teaching, in the widest application of the practice, furthers both the development and individuation of both the teachers and those learning. In this way, the quality of teachers and the dedication of students is not only the most immediately beneficial but also an essential component of creative evolution as collective individuation. This creative evolution within the pedagogical moment is beautifully articulated in verse by Rilke (1924/1992, p.236) when he wrote, "Take your well-disciplined strengths/ and stretch them between two/ opposing poles. Because inside human beings/ is where God learns."

REFERENCES

Adams, D. (2005). *The ultimate hitchhiker's guide: Five complete novels and one story.* Gramercy Books.
Alinsky, S. D. (1971). *Rules for radicals: A practical primer for realistic radicals.* Vintage Books.
Bergson, H. (1965/1902). *Creative evolution.* Modern Library.
Bly, R. (1977). *The sibling society.* Random House.
Campbell, J. (1949). *The hero with a thousand faces* (3rd ed.). New World Library.
Dewey, J. (1934). *Art as experience.* The Berkley Publishing Group.

Dewey, J. (1990). *The school and society: The child and the curriculum.* University of Chicago Press.

Donne, J. (1959). Devotions upon emergent occasions and seuerall steps in my Sicknes. In *John Donne Devotions upon emergent occasions together with Death's Duel.* The University of Michigan Press. (Original work published 1624).

Frankl, V. E. (1973). *The doctor and the soul: From psychotherapy to logotherapy.* Random House.

Frankl, V. E. (2015). *Man's search for meaning* (Gift ed.). Beacon Press.

Freire, P. (1968). *Pedagogy of the oppressed.* The Seabury Press.

Freire, P. (1997). *Pedagogy of the heart.* Continuum International Publishing Group.

Greene, R. (2000). *The 48 laws of power.* Penguin Books.

Guggenbühl-Craig, A. (1971). *Power in the helping professions.* Spring Publications, Inc.

Hillman, J. (1995). *Kinds of power: A guide to its intelligent uses.* Currency Doubleday.

Johnson, R. (2017). *Inner gold: Understanding psychological projection.* Chiron Publications.

Jung, C. G. (1966). Psychotherapy and a philosophy of life (R. F. C. Hull, Trans.). In H. Read et al. (Eds.), *The collected works of C. G. Jung* (Vol. 16, 2nd ed.). Retrieved from http://www.proquest.com (Original work published 1946)

Jung, C. G. (1959). The face-to-face interview. In *C.G. Jung speaking: Interviews and encounters*, pp. 424–39. Bollingen Paperbacks, 1977.

Jung, C. G. (1970). *The collected works of C. G. Jung: Vol. 14. Mysterium coniunctionis* (R. F. C. Hull, Trans.) (H. Read et al., Eds.). Princeton University Press. (Original work published 1955–1956)

Jung, C. G. (1969). A study in the process of individuation (R. F. C. Hull, Trans.). In H. Read et al. (Series Eds.), *The collected works of C. G. Jung* (Vol. 9, pt. 1, 2nd. ed., pp. 290–354). Princeton University Press. (Original work published 1950)

Kell, K. (2021a). Archetypal "vocationing": Being a teacher, healer, and artist at work. In C. Mayes, S. Persing, & C. Schumacher (Eds.), *New visions and new voices: Extending the principles of archetypal pedagogy to include a variety of venues, issues, and projects* (pp. 127–38). Rowman & Littlefield.

Kell, K. (2021b). Transcending the power complex: A typological use of active imagination. Personality Type in Depth, April 2021. Retrieved from https://typeindepth.org/2021/04/active-imagination-to-transcend-the-power-complex/

Kopp, S. (1977). *Back to one.* Science and Behavior Books, Inc.

Mayes, C. (2005). *Teaching mysteries: Foundations of spiritual pedagogy.* University Press of America.

Mayes, C. (2019). *Developing the whole student: New horizons in holistic education.* Rowman and Littlefield Press.

Piaget, J. (1969). *The psychology of the child.* Basic Books.

Pullman, P. (2007). *The subtle knife*, in *His dark materials.* Random House. (Original published 1997)

Rilke, R. M. (1992). Just as the winged energy of delight. In R. Bly, J. Hillman & M. Meade (Eds.), *The rag and bone shop of the heart* (p. 236). Harper Perennial.

Tzu, S. (2003). *The art of war: Complete texts and commentaries*, trans. T. Cleary. Shambhala Publications, Inc.

Watts, A. (1989). *The book: On the taboo against knowing who you are.* Vintage Books Random House.

Chapter 8

Education for Integration—
Not Annihilation

Jacquelyn Rinaldi

STRIVING FOR INTEGRATION, NOT ANNIHILATION

Integration

For C. J. Jung integration is a way to describe wholeness. This process is something that we work on throughout our lives, deepening integration as we traverse the challenges that inevitably arise through a lifetime. As one learns to hold the light and the dark aspect of oneself with a sense of curiosity and humility, integration proceeds, and this is, as Jung describes it, part of the individuation process. Individuation is the process by which a person begins to see through their projections and complexes as well as looking into the shadow. It is the process of finding out who one truly is amidst the unrefined, raw, underdeveloped, and dark elements that reside within. Individuation creates a stronger personality, one who is less susceptible to *mass-mindedness*, which Jung describes as a type of loyalty to the cult of the State (Jung, 1970b).

The individuation process allows a person to see themselves and in turn the world with more clarity and then interact with greater effectiveness. Jung explains, "A man who understands and comes to terms with the different aspects of his inner being is enabled to live life more completely" (1983, p. 24). From this, it follows, Jung announced, that "anyone who has insight into his own actions, and has thus found access to the unconscious, involuntarily exercises an influence on his environment" (1970b, p. 303).

It is difficult for most to look at the qualities of Self that they do not wish to see, but this pushing away only makes those dark aspects stronger.

This denial allows those aspects of personality to grow widely within the shadow, beneath conscious awareness. When energy lives in the shadow, self-sabotaging behaviors often come from nowhere and feel like fate. Yet, there is always a choice; the reactivity is not fated. The self-sabotaging behaviors are a manifestation of the qualities of Self that are not granted a voice. When those elements are given a voice, as happens when one courageously chooses to see what lives in the shadow, one navigates the difficult yet rewarding path of individuation.

As one continuously works to shine more light into the shadow, greater consciousness is realized and that reduces the reactivity from within. This engenders more peace and balance in one's life. As Jung instructs us, "Only the man who can consciously assent to the power of the inner voice becomes a personality" (Jung, 1983, p. 19). It is through the archetype of the Self that we begin to move toward the collective unconscious. The door to the numinous opens as one looks within.

Knowing that every human being is made from both light and dark aspects can help us face the reality of our own shadow, and we learn to balance the two polarities rather than denying the existence of anything outside of our personal ideal. The balancing of the two polarities is integration. As Jung describes it, "I can master their polarity only by freeing myself from them by contemplating both, and so reaching a middle position. Only there am I no longer at the mercy of the opposites" (Jung, 1970a, p. 464). Jung called this union of opposites the *transcendent function.*

It is easy to believe we are becoming God-like in our thinking processes and to fancy that *my* truth is the superior truth. One's perspective can so easily seem to oneself to be the totality of what could be, but in reality, this perspective shows one is caught by their own narcissistic delusion. One cannot conceivably see the totality of all possibilities; that is the perspective of God, not that of humanity. When one sees their truth with a capital T, that *Truth* becomes the only approved narrative as if delivered by God. This dangerous and unchecked perspective is a result of the shadow captaining the ship.

It is humility that allows one to see that there will always be a greater frontier to explore and deeper insight to uncover. As T. S. Eliot (1971, p. 165) wrote, "The only wisdom we can hope to acquire is the wisdom of humility. Humility is endless." Humility brings authentic curiosity about the frontier that lies beyond one's current perspective. It is accurate empathy and humility that encourage self-reflection. Accurate empathy is not a weakness; it is not blindly accommodating or pleasing others.

Accurate empathy is assertive and strong and at the same time it holds a softness for understanding the hardship others face as well as one's own. Accurate empathy does not take responsibility where it is unwarranted. In fact, accurate empathy would not rob another of the opportunity to learn from the natural consequence of life by taking responsibility for their condition. As she develops more accurate empathy, a person also cultivates the skill to self-reflect and see more clearly the aspects of Self that she is not particularly proud of. Accurate empathy and humility foster responsibility because a person sees herself and others more clearly and that clarity will not allow her to make others responsible for what becomes manifest in her life.

Humility does not indicate a lack of confidence; on the contrary humility is strong yet fluid. In humility the edges of understanding remain permeable, knowing there are always greater frontiers to explore. When the edges become hardened, curiosity dies. One is no longer open to the numinous or to creativity. One must step into the unknown to truly find innovation. It is the numinous that reminds us that we do not see the totality; when we experience the numinous, we understand that something bigger than us is at play (Jung, 1970a).

When she recognizes that the shadow elements exist within her as much as they exist within her enemy, she opens the door to confront those difficult aspects more readily within herself. When she sees that the shadow is part of everyone, she is more likely to approach the parts she does not wish to see about herself with curiosity rather than with denial, fear, or distain. When she remains fearful of those dark parts within herself, projection becomes a routine coping strategy because she believes the problem and responsibility consistently reside outside of her. Projection fosters her artificial personality because she blames the world around her for its darkness and remains blind to her own. This self-blindness leads to dysfunctional thinking patterns and neurosis as the ego seeks to protect conscious awareness from seeing this darkness that is growing within her Shadow.

Jung elaborates on this point: "A man cannot get rid of himself in favor of an artificial personality without punishment" (Jung, 1983, p. 95). As she sees her own capacity for darkness, a person sees herself more honestly. And that clarity also allows her to see the world from a sharper perspective. She is no longer seeing the darkness as something that is *out there* which needs to be eliminated but something that is part of her wholeness, as it is for each of us. Darkness is not something that can be eliminated; it is something that must be made conscious. The shadow does not signify evil. It is the human capacity that incorporates both the negative aspects of who we are and our unrealized or underdeveloped potential (Jung, 1969).

Annihilation

If on the other hand one, fights a battle to eliminate the evil *out there,* she becomes caught by her own projection or self-righteous indignation as she believes everyone thinks like she thinks, and those outside that perspective are wrong. Jung teaches, "the projection carries the *fear* which we involuntarily and secretly feel for our own evil on the other side and considerably increases the formidableness of this threat" (1970b, p. 279). To become conscious of one's shadow "involves recognizing the dark aspects of the personality as present and real. This act is the essential condition for any kind of self-knowledge, and it therefore, as a rule, meets with considerable resistance" (Jung, 1968, p. 8). The often-misnamed "evil" is simply the opposite side of the same coin. We cannot eliminate parts of the whole and seeking to do so will only make the darkness denser.

As theories and perspectives become the one and only right view, we limit and censor the potential for growth. This has political as well as personal consequences, as Jung was often quick to point out. For, when certain perspectives become legitimized by the state as certain *Fact*, with a capital F, ideas that differ are shamed, ridiculed, and silenced. This gives ultimate, *hegemonic* power to the State as it becomes the one and only authority on *truth* (Gramsci, 1991).

Jung declares, "The life of the individual is not determined solely by the ego and its opinions or by social factors, but quite as much, if not more, by a transcendent authority" (Jung, 1970b, p. 257). The transcendent authority becomes the state, and the goal of education and enlightenment is for the individual to function as an effective part of the state forwarding the prescribed narratives (Jung, 1970b). This is the annihilation of the essence of humanity as the masses robotically follow what is taught. The essence of humanity is the inner journey—to become one's best self. When the deeper understanding of the inner journey is denied, individuation becomes a canceled project of the past. Jung insists that when such a state of affairs exists, then

> [t]he state takes the place of God; that is why, seen from this angle, the socialist dictatorships are religions and State slavery is a form of worship. But the religious function cannot be dislocated and falsified in this way without giving rise to secret doubts, which are immediately repressed so as to avoid conflict with the prevailing trend towards mass-mindedness. The result, as always in such cases, is overcompensation in the form of *fanaticism*, which in its turn is used as a weapon for stamping out the least flicker of opposition. Free opinion is stifled and moral decision ruthlessly suppressed, on the plea that the end justifies the means, even the vilest. The policy of the State is exalted to a creed, the leader or party boss becomes a demigod beyond good and evil, and his votaries are honoured as heroes, martyrs, apostles, missionaries. There is only *one* truth and besides it no other. It is sacrosanct and above criticism. Anyone who thinks differently is a heretic, who, as we know from history is threatened with all manner of unpleasant things. (1970b, p. 259)

Clearly, this is not an environment for growth or development; on the contrary, this violent thinking pattern is vicious and abusive. It cultivates mass-mindedness or group-think among its constituents. The masses remain stuck and alarmingly blinded within the confines of their own projection as determined by the influence of the state. Prophetically, Jung makes it clear that "[w]henever social conditions of this type develop on a large scale, the road to tyranny lies open and the freedom of the individual turns into spiritual and physical slavery" (1970b, p. 277).

The narrative that often arises as blame toward an entire political party or social group for the problems within a community, country, or culture is a *collective projection*. The collective unconscious is fed by each of us. As more of humanity reaches a peaceful resolution within themselves, they feed the collective unconscious the same peaceful resolve. When the masses are caught by complexes and unconscious pulls from the Shadow, the collective is darkened by that influence.

Integration in Pedagogy

The archetypal educator is called to teach learners to sit with the unknown and discover from within their own truth. This allows these students to compose the song that lives inside them. It is educators who inspire learners to see beyond the prescribed narratives. The student's task should be to find the song that lives inside each of them. Educators should foster the tools supporting growth and creativity so students gain confidence and wisdom to sing that song to the world. The stewardship of developing minds does not mean passing on ideology; it means offering opportunities for learners to explore their own inner pulse and discover where their truth lies to facilitate students growing into the best version of who they are.

As students arrive at their own understanding through the interaction of scholastics and self-exploration, they gain self-esteem, courage, and a passion for what lives inside them—their song. When that song is realized they will have made their education meaningful. When these self-affirming qualities are instilled in our students, we will have done something to move the world toward growth. As Jung insists, "the value of a community depends on the spiritual and moral stature of the individuals composing it" (1970b, p. 262). The further down the road of individuation one travels, the greater one's capacity for brilliance. This journey toward greater self-understanding can and should be inspired through education.

It is a fallacy as well as arrogant for an instructor or an institution to believe they hold all the answers—the God-complex at work. Institutions and instructors speak of critical thinking yet condemn any view outside of the State prescribed narrative. It is projection when as a teacher I spout the importance of critical thinking yet assume that everyone in the classroom holds the same view as I, shaming any thought outside of the *approved* view before a discussion even begins. This common experience within the classroom extinguishes critical thinking, developing lower-order robotic thought processes in learners as they become disciples of the State.

The devotees will value the *approved truth* and theories as the single correct path toward righteousness and will *themselves* then take on the charge to condemn those who fall outside of that prescribed ideology. Questioning the approved thought is not a part of the plan and is driven away by fear of creativity, innovation, and critical thinking, precisely what Dewey (1916) warned against as that kind of totalitarian anti-education that is tantamount to propaganda and thus inimical to a democracy. Jung warns, "[T]o rope the individual into a social organization and reduce him to a condition of diminished responsibility, instead of raising him out of the torpid, mindless mass and making clear to him that *he* is the one important factor and that the salvation of the world consists in the salvation of the individual soul" (1970b, p. 276). As more learners find the courage to embark on the individuation process the more whole the collective unconscious becomes, and that indeed will do something to change the current fragmented state of the world.

The only way to develop innovation and creativity is to allow learners to express themselves freely. The educational forum needs to be a place where it is safe enough to be wrong some of the time—without fear of being shamed or canceled. Going out on a limb and experiencing what *creating* an idea feels like is how we learn what lives inside; it is how we define our own truth. A totalitarian archetype, the shadow side of the archetypes of true leadership, has plagued academia and has become a grave barrier toward advancement. Institutions are not creating minds that think critically and creatively. It is creating androids who do as they are told. These educated elites are more susceptible to control as they become leaders under the pull of mass-mindedness, feeling entitled to patrol others who question the prescribed order of thought. When that happens, the teacher becomes an ideological enforcer, not an open-minded liberator.

Instructors can begin to facilitate a transition out of the current mass-minded model by inviting a more inquiring relationship with the unconscious. This fosters the development of passionate, innovative, and creative thinkers who have the courage and capacity to show up in inspiring ways. The instructor who facilitates this depth psychological approach to pedagogy that Mayes (2020) advocates for encourages the learner to embark on their own journey of self-understanding and individuation. As each of us becomes more aware of who we are and what drives our inner constitution, we make choices that are more congruent with what we believe we should be doing. We experience less cognitive dissonance, and that creates stronger self-esteem and greater resilience.

As Jung teaches, "if the individual is not truly regenerated in spirit, society cannot be either, for society is the sum total of individuals in need of redemption" (1970b, p. 276). As more individuals have a stake in the game because they are living and working from a place of inspiration and passion, we will have moved the world toward wholeness, no longer teaching learners to mechanically reproduce the current approved version of the truth. Jung avers that "it is always a question of treating one single individual only and not ten thousand, when the trouble one takes would ostensibly have more impressive results, though one knows well enough that nothing has happened at all unless the individual changes" (1970b, p. 302).

When we have a society that has embarked on the road to individuation, opening the door to the path of becoming their best self, we will have made strides toward moving the collective unconscious in the direction of a more peaceful and whole position. What wholeness brings to each of us is greater emotional intelligence and functioning which enhances the experience of life. A fragmented psyche is more susceptible to control, conflict, and reactivity because of distorted thinking patterns and perceptions.

One of the goals of therapy is to teach people to live in reality, which means it is going to be uncomfortable as one learns to see past their limited perspective. As educators we also take this role to encourage students to sit in that discomfort in order to expand their current perception. Growth comes from thinking differently, from seeing the horizon beyond the bend, and this expansion of perception is hard work. But as teachers inspire learners to answer the call to their hero's journey, they teach students to stoke their own fires of curiosity, depth, and greater understanding. And that realizes the true purpose of education, which is to be the breeding ground for innovation—the site for integration of the total person, not her annihilation as a mere creature of the State.

REFERENCES

Dewey, J. (1916). *Democracy and education.* The Free Press.

Eliot, T.S. (1971). *The complete poems and plays of T. S. Eliot.* Harcourt, Brace, and Jovanovich.

Gramsci, A. (1997). *Prison notebooks.* Columbia University Press.

Jung, C. G. (1968). *The collected works of C. G. Jung: Vol. 9, pt. 2. Aion: Researches into the phenomenology of the self* (R. F. C. Hull, Trans.) (H. Read et al., Eds.). Princeton University Press. (Original work published 1951). https://doi.org/10.1515/9781400851058

Jung, C. G. (1969). Psychology and religion. In H. Read et al. (Eds.), *The collected works of C. G. Jung: Vol. 11. Psychology and religion* (2nd ed., pp. 3–105). Princeton University Press. (Original work published 1940). https://doi.org/10.1515/9781400850983.3

Jung, C. G. (1970a). Good and evil in analytical psychology (R. F. C. Hull, Trans.). In H. Read et al. (Eds.), *The collected works of C. G. Jung: Vol. 10. Civilization in transition* (2nd ed., pp. 456–68). Princeton University Press. (Original work published 1959). https://doi.org/10.1515/9781400850976.456

Jung, C. G. (1970b). The undiscovered self (present and future) (R. F. C. Hull, Trans.). In H. Read et al. (Eds.), *The collected works of C. G. Jung: Vol. 10. Civilization in transition* (2nd ed., pp. 247–305). Princeton University Press. (Original work published 1957). https://doi.org/10.1515/9781400850976.247

Jung, C. G. (1983). *The essential Jung* (A. Storr, Ed.). Princeton University Press.

Mayes, C. (2020). *Archetype, culture, and the individual in education: The three pedagogical narratives.* Routledge.

Chapter 9

The Poet as an Archetypal Teacher (in Unteachable Times)

The Poetry of Kyle Jankowski

Clifford Mayes

One must be existentially specific right out of the gate in discussing Kyle Jankowski, for he defies generalizations. He is *sui generis.* This is not to say that certain cultural and ideological categories do not fit him. Of course, they do. They fit us all. But as the existentialist motto ran (and Jankowski, never one to be trendy, has a foot in that now lamentably forgotten school of philosophy and art), "Existence precedes essence." This is true even of those "essential" cultural categories and dispositions in Jankowski and his poetry that are so centrally important to him: Polish American from the heart of the Rust Belt, Catholic, psychotherapist, conservative (but in a radical way) and radical (but in a conservative way).

Those categories both clarify who he is yet also occlude it. He does not try to be "representative" of anyone except himself. He does not set out to "appeal" to any particular group. Indeed, there are few groups on our conflicted politico-cultural landscape that escape his notice. In Jankowski personally and professionally, ideological and religious categories interweave in an unlikely multiplexity that also, paradoxically, underline his typicality in our radically multicultural epoch.

It is a sharp wind that blows over the Carpathian Range of his poetry, and it is refreshing, as such winds are, because they are not heavy with the humidity of currying favor with the reader. Kyle is one of those people who says what he means and means what he says. He is urbane and kind, but he does not let politeness stand in the way of truth when truth must be spoken.

In reading him, therefore, you will be too engrossed by his poetry to stop, or you will feel too threatened by it to go on. You will not be anywhere in the middle. Kyle Jankowski is an all-or-nothing artist. He simply does not have the time for "messing with Mr. In-Between," as the old song from World War II (a period that fascinates this voracious reader of history) went. It would cut too much into his time for poetry, which he balances against his work as a psychotherapist with a Jungian-oriented practice.

For instance, in one of his poems, "Why the Union Worker's Son Wouldn't Buy American," Jankowski explains his reluctance to *be* a "good American" by *buying* American. It is because of the following:

> Nordic featured anorexic dolls living the California dream
> Have their plastic parts attached in China, while the girls they are based on
> Have their plastic parts attached in Dr. Chen's L.A. office.

To be sure, this proletarian polemic against the rich and famous fits his identity as a Polish blue-collar Catholic from the rough-and-tumble Rust Belt at its rustiest.

What that assemblage of categorical markers can *not* prepare you for, however, is his tender, Chopinesque homage (swept by penitent, pensive chords) in "Crone Poetry" to an aged poetess standing in front of a rudely disinterested class. It is a lamentation for how little her brutish students (including himself) have seen and honored her for the presence and preciousness she is as the embodiment of the archetypally feminine. She is made even more beautiful by her advancing age as she sadly plays her final role on the mortal stage to mere groundlings. She is also beautiful in her role as a dying avatar of an expiring aesthetic of loveliness. The class all but mocks her; they deny and deride the psychospiritual nourishment she graciously proffers, the ritual in words she would enact with them but that they dismiss as eccentricity. Because she is not "cool," they are cruel. With chuckles and rolled eyes, they caricature her classes as just an old woman's

> "Poetry club."
> That's what some snickered and moaned,
> Refusing her nourishment.
> Too cowardly to join the ritual, including me.
> Secretly, I revered her bravery, revered *her*:
> A real Crone, but no one knew what she meant.
> Too much fear, agitation, impatience.
> We were young professionals.

No. The first poem does not prepare you for the second.

But this is Jankowski's world: an ongoing dialectic, a clash but also communion of opposites: unapologetically conservative yet also an archetypical Chicago-radical in the Jane Addams and Carl Sandburg tradition; point-man on any Jungian adventure of any psychospiritual moment yet one who tells his beads on an Eastern-European rosary; in touch with the inner-feminine yet fierce as Dirty Harry pounding a few home-truths into an entitled punk who never learned the truth at home from his morally vagrant parents—the kind of kids he spends a lot of time with in his clinical practice and as a co-director of the Center for Change and healing, an adult and pediatric clinic near Chicago.

Let us now turn to two of his poems, which will give you a genuine feel for Jankowski because they are so steeped in the principal—and always principled—images and motifs, issues and tropes that inform his upcoming volume: *Reflections of a Polish Sun.* They are "Our Lady's Cloak" an "Under God's Windows." These poems—in their exquisite explications of Polish culture, its enduring but troubled marriage with American culture in the Polish American experience, its Catholic commitments and political mysticisms, its encounter with some of the great historical issues of the last 100 years along with its celebration of small and humble things, will serve to orient the reader to fully enter into other poems in the book.

They range from (1) "This Is How They Will Come for Us," with the poet as cultural critic who wryly notes that "[i]n the free market we all trade / Privacy for emoji, / Anonymity for 'connectivity.' Click agree or you cannot participate. . . . / What membership did we sign for? / This is how they will come for us"; (2) "The Shadow of Addiction," written by Jankowski the poet-therapist who understands the spiritual roots of substance abuse: "Drowning in feelings, because you never learned how to swim, / Drink it down, *spirits* help you float"; (3) "*Si Vas Pacem Para Bellum*," featuring Jankowski as the geopolitical realist who, as a historically-learned Pole, understands that force must sometimes be met with force, and therefore in tones and terms that are bound to rub the politically correct the wrong way, announces that "we do not consult Buddha, but gladly invite Sun Tzu, Sobieski and Pilsudski to council / Our motto: *Less mindfulness, more marksmanship*. Better marksmanship *through* mindfulness. . . . Let meditators wander in the cloudy tantric. / We localize the laser-focus tactic"; and, in "Ovens," whose title is an allusion to the homely virtues of Poland, literally "edifying," truth made savory in Polish cuisine, but staring still in horror at the ovens in the camps in Poland's Majdanek, Auschwitz, and Treblinka that set half an ancient race on fire and almost burned it out of existence. The unusual presence of five stoves and ovens in her grandmother's kitchen.

> Circled around the five modern hearths in a
> Ritual of nourishing,

Arguing and remembering—
Old recipes, how so-and-so used to make it.
Zadie and Bubbe's house is preternaturally quiet.
Today as she walks through the lifeless rooms
The large burnt-out sculpture still looms in the back yard after all
these years
Staring at a burnt Trojan horse with old patchwork quilts haphaz-
ardly tossed over it
As if wild European folk-patterned-cloth would camouflage this
Ten-foot-tall, charred beast, presiding over the garden shed.
Staring at the sculpture with a cousin, she remarks
On the state of grandmother's home.
"Everyone knows what happened in the war. . . . "
"Yes," she allows, hollow-eyed.
"But I cannot remember
What happened after."

Each category interacts with each—consistently but also idiosyncratically—
at a sort of 81 degree angle. For although devout, Jankowski is never dog-
matic; and although conservative in many of his manifestations, it is with
a counter-cultural passion that should leave the self-proclaimed "radical"
wondering about his own disruptive *bona fides* compared to Jankowski's jar-
ring contestations.

A NOTE ON AESTHETICS (WITH SPECIAL REFERENCE TO JANKOWSKI)

The immature poet is inchoate. He rushes toward new themes in every poem,
tripping over himself in a mad dash to be (or *seem* to be) novel at every turn.
He misconstrues the p calling as "novelty in all cases and at any cost!" He
is a caricature of the Romantic ethos and aesthetic, for he fails to establish
an orbit around the core themes that comprise the planet in whose gravity he
is presently drawn, and will continue to be drawn, in a soft-landing on some
ancient ground of his being—of Being Itself. It is the place both before and
beyond "place" where the subjective and the objective merge, a place of
ontological "standing" but also phenomenological fluidity, Wallace Stevens's
"mere being."

As in the calculus with its "asymptotic limits," the poet, a psychospiritual
mathematician of the transcendent, is always approximating infinity but
never fully attaining it. That would be to be a saint, not a poet, and despite his
Catholicism, it is as a poet that Mr. Jankowski lives—as a poet, that is, and
as a psychotherapist, his two, highly interactive callings, for reading poetry

with his analysands is often a part if his "treatment" of them, just as there is a certain "curative" effect in immersing oneself in *his* poetry.

At any rate, his poems are the chronicle of these asymptotic descent-ascents, and, in a sense, *are* the goal. For Jankowski, poetry is apotheosis, and we miss the poetry, not to mention missing the man, if we try to sidestep the "metaphysical" in it and him—using that now neglected branch of philosophy term both *philosophically* (there is simply no sidestepping the fact that Jankowski is a religious poet) and also *historically* (like the 17th-century "Metaphysical Poets," Jankowski often achieves his effect through John Donne's technique of deploying "disparate images by violence yoked together."

It is not so much novelty, then, that makes for greatness in poetry, and it is not novelty that portends greatness in this newly visible poet. Bad poetry can be novel. A good deal of what gets published these days shows that clearly enough. Thus, although he *is* novel, as mentioned above in the way he approaches his themes, it is Jankowski's consistency and economy *in* his themes, his incremental, unflagging divestiture of ego in order to find the timeless Self and to do so in a consciousness of the past that leads to a radical interrogation of the present directing us toward a principled future, that impresses. This is consistent with Eliot's aesthetic as laid out in "Tradition and the Individual Talent" (Eliot, 2021). It is also a quintessentially Jungian project, and Jankowski is a Jungian-oriented psychotherapist—already an act of defiance on his part as an MSW of the prestigious but normative University of Chicago School of Social Work.

And this thematic focus and resolve generally revolves around a few choice themes in a poet's work that he recursively treats—from new angles and in new cadences, of course, across his poems—but in unity and fixity of purpose throughout his poetic career. They often, themselves, organize around one or two themes. For Mr. Jankowski, there are two interactive motifs that power his prodigious output: (1) his infrastructural Catholicism, drenched in his devotion to the Black Madonna); and (2) his identity as a native son of the American Rust Belt, whose ears are always abuzz with the droning (now joyful, now mournful) of the hurdy-gurdy of his spiritual heartland/homeland: Poland.

Nowhere is the first motif more clearly on display than in "Our Lady's Cloak."

KHRUSHCHEV'S CONSTRUCTIONS,
FOUCAULT'S DECONSTRUCTIONS, AND
THE BLACK MADONNA'S CLOAK

Our Lady's Cloak
You are all alone now,
In your isolated redoubt—but still
Their propaganda is blasting in your head.

The barbarians are at the gates
Ready to drag you into the virtual Colosseum
Of public opinion
And lash you raw before feeding you
To press corps and false friends—
The lions that ate Ignatius.

Wrap yourself in Our Lady's Cloak.
Don't let your sanity be smashed into shards,
Shattered grist on the mind's millstone.
Our Lady's Cloak
Will protect the heartland's borders

From brutish invaders, love's infidels, and
Mental bolshevism: "Now, we take you
To our scheduled broadcast on College-SPAN:
"This tribunal will come to order!"

Maria, Mater Dei, ora pro nobis.
"This meeting sits to determine the fate of those
Who speak against our glorious rhetorical revolution:
The erasure of genuine subjective experience
By the dollar-store eraser of Political Correctness."

Maria, Regina, ora pro nobis.

"But first, the Politburo Commissar on Intersectionality
Will lead us
In a non-denominational prayer of non-being."

Mary, Gratia Plena, pray for us now,
And at the hour of our death.
Shelter us in your cloak
As we count its lilies into untroubled dreamtime.

Although Jankowski is not fundamentally a poet in the Romantic tradition of Wordsworth and Keats but, truth be told, is more in the Classical vein and moves more in the classical venues of Dryden (especially in Jankowski's caustic cuts at the reigning elite and their "culture of cool" with its fashionable moral bankruptcy; one thinks of Dryden's "Rape of the Lock"), there is a hefty admixture of the Romantic voice resonating in his work. "You are alone now."

Here is the poet as Romantic hero—wandering "lonely as a cloud" in Wordsworth's poem of the same name while defying the Gods as in Shelley's "Prometheus." Yet, Jankowski's introversion is as much responsible for his solitary redoubt as is any possible Romantic influence from, say, Coleridge, pining poetically away in "This Lime Tree Bower, My Prison." And it is not against a heavenly aristocracy that Jankowski inveighs, as Shelley has Prometheus do, but to Heaven's Queen that Jankowski appeals, as a Catholic specially may.

This, Jankowski, like his co-religionist and similarly trenchant cultural critic Andrew Sullivan, sees as a major cause as well as symptom of all of this the iconoclasm of postmodernism. There, nothing is sacred and everything is susceptible to a thoroughgoing "hermeneutics of suspicion," which sees every text and social institution as a covert attempt by an invisible power elite to control us from its privileged but camouflaged positions of its power-mad, deep political bases of control. This will be a control not only of institutions but of language itself, all of which must be taken apart to reveal the worm in every apple and replaced with politically correct language. This is called "the hermeneutics of suspicion" (Ricoeur, 1990).

As he so often does, Jankowski turns to Our Lady to make sense of this mess and to find refuge from it.

Agni Parthene

(Rejoice, ode of the seraphim/ and joy of the archangels. Rejoice, O peace; Rejoice, O joy/ and haven of salvation. O bridal chamber of the Word/ unfading, fragrant blossom. Rejoice, delight of paradise/ Rejoice, life everlasting.")*

> Though we may seek His guidance in the Dark Night,
> She claims us, enfolding all in her mantle
>
> In times when small sacred things are profaned
> Her presence blooms fullest.
> In the Bridal Chamber of the Word,
> With Her as witness,

We marry ourselves to Truth,
Holding close to our hearts
The Flower of Incorruption,
To inspire all Her children.
Holy Mary of Perpetual Succor
Outshining Persephone, Hekate, Hera
Running beneath us as we plunge into the underworld
Of our era.

Here is a thoroughgoing critique of the postmodern point of view (if that movement can be said to *have* a point of view). Yet, despite his general dislike of the postmodern view and, despite his marked and courageous anti-postmodernism, he shares some of it—but with a difference. The difference, and it is huge, is two-fold.

The first is that Mr. Jankowski finds political correctness rhetorically ridiculous, intellectually indefensible, and ethically odious. Second, unlike the postmodern crew, Jankowski believes that something good can come of it all, that awareness of it can, through collective minding of it and concerted action against it, lead to a restoration of classical democratic values and processes. For Jankoswki, decidedly *not* a member of the New Left, grand narratives of constitutional federalism are not insipid but inspiring, Jankowski believes that their light may shine us a path forward to a new pluralistic democracy, where civilized discourse, not snide sniping and outright excoriation, prevails.

It is the linguistic totalitarianism of the far-Left's political correctness (Jankowski is equally contemptuous of the far-Right's moralistic diatribes) that Jankowski is referring to in his ironic notice of the "glorious rhetorical revolution," whose goal, which it is Jankowski's purpose to debunk through poetry, is to educate us to this fact. The poet's pedagogical role is nowhere clearer than here. The postmodern goal, in point of fact, is not to liberate people but to corral their every thought by determining which words are acceptable and which are not, what language we are now legally compelled to use and which to avoid—and all in the service of a far-Left program of ethno-sexual politics (or, again, the opposite but equal outrage of the far-Right's imposition of a viciously naïve "purity").

For, whether it rests upon alt-Leftism or alt-Rightism, the danger is that through covert and overt means the State will finally occupy the beachheads of one's very cognition, straighten out all the wrinkles of difference until the populace is flawless in its bovine complicity, and thus succeed in bringing to pass what both Orwell and Huxley prophetically warned us could well become the Waterloo of humanity—namely, the phenomenological fascism of the total state; "the erasure," as Jankowski baldly and boldly puts it, "of genuine subjective experience." That we are already pretty far down that "road to serfdom" is one of Jankowski's greatest hues and cries (Hayek, 1944).

Not surprisingly, then, as an antidote to the iconoclasm of postmodernism, it is to an icon that Jankowski (re)turns, in the Dante-esque *media res* of his life at 37. In liturgical lyricism, reminiscent of Eliot in "Ash Wednesday," he invokes *Maria* as *Regina* and *Mater Dei*. She, *Gratia Plena*, will serve the poet as he, the quintessential Pole militant appealing to her as his gentle General, takes up his prosodic and imagistic sword, to serve the Virgin—his true redoubt, her cloak his protection and beneficent weapon against both the edicts of the *Politburo* and the counterintuitive insistences and linguistic laughability of the academy's fatal fling with postmodernism.

We see this linkage in this poem in the poet's conflation of an official Soviet pronouncement with the hegemony of "Political Correctness" about not only what may be *said* but even *thought* ("Their propaganda is blasting in your head"; "sanity . . . smashed into shards . . . on the mind's millstone"). And it all comes to a culmination on campus, where every kind of intellectual and libidinal excess is allowed, even encouraged. And it is worthwhile noting here that not only in his archetypally pedagogical poetics but in his historical concern with the devolution of educational institutions, Jankowski's work can be read as an almost journalistic exposition of the sorry state of affairs in current scholastic theories and practices, where, in the name of academic freedom, any kind of errant nonsense can prevail.

For, as Dostoyevsky has Ivan Karamasov say in "The Grand Inquisitor" section of *The Brothers Karamazov*, where there is no God and truth goes a-glimmering, nothing is forbidden, everything is allowed. Everything, that is, except that simplest and most necessary of things—an ethic rooted in an authentic ontological commitment.

Something that is "Ultimate" for that person (Tillich, 1983)—a "fiduciary commitment" (Ricoeur, 1985) that is strong but also open to being educated by others' fiduciary commitments.

Jankowski does not think it too much to ask professors to actually believe in something, to enter into dialogue with others who believe in something, and for all involved to have both the humility and courage to be changed by others' beliefs, just as one hopes they will be changed by one's own. In short, Jankowski forwards the truly outrageous notion in our fractious, obsessively argumentative times that civilized discourse, not political shouting matches, should set the tone and define the purpose of academic life (Mayes, 2020). In this as in so much else in this historically sensitive poet, Jankowski is on firm historical ground.

In the first universities, beginning with the University of Bologna in 1046, one was called a professor because he "professed" a faith in God, in light of which his scholarship was carried out. Almost a millennium later, "professor" too often connotes just the opposite—someone whose dubious expertise—defined not by what it can do but what it can undo—lies in desacralizing any and everything, extinguishing "the hermeneutics of faith and hope" (Homans, 1995) with the brackish, factious postmodern water of riotous intellectual living in the hermeneutics of suspicion, which smells a rat even in the most sacred of things.

The university thereby becomes an official propagandistic organ where students are miseducated into political conformance in the anti-ethics of the New Left. It is a colossal betrayal of the mission of the university, a pedagogical collapse, which Jankowski's poetry sets out to identify and remediate through the truly radical autonomy of language in poetry itself. This is another aspect of the poet as pedagogue; and even more as *archetypal* pedagogue when, as in Jankowski, the poet so often and generally quite successfully aims to constellate his poetry as a numinous zone.

In this manner, the poet becomes a pedagogue of intellectual liberty and spiritual affirmation. Jankowski exhorts the professor to again "profess" something of intellectual charm, historical awareness, and ethical moment. The revolution Jankowski would bring about is thus in large measure an educational one. He attends closely to Shelley's thrilling insistence that "the poet is the unacknowledged legislator he of the world" and extends the poet's role to being the unacknowledged *teacher* of the world, too, which accounts for the occasional hortatory note in Jankowski, which, admittedly, Jankowski can sometimes take too far.

It also accounts for why so much of his poetry is not primarily a private thought process that the poet is letting the reader into (as in the Confessional poets); nor is it public theorizing in poetic form about some ideological imperative or another (as in the official state poetry of Soviet communism). Rather, it is a conversation in which the poet assays to educate the reader, and, like all great teaching, this happens on a one-to-one basis, with the teacher in an I-Thou relationship with his student—or, in Jankowski's case, the poet with his reader, both caught up in a sometimes fierce but always friendly dialogue—"dialogical partners" (Buber, 1965).

The final irony in the assault on the individual and her subjectivity (and Jankowski is a master ironist, as Poles have perforce learned to be in their harsh history) is that Romanticism—originally an accentuation of "subjective experience"—led us a perplexing route (but then again, "history has many cunning and deceiving passages," said Eliot) from subjective experience as the liberation of man in the erasure of God to subjective experience made a slave to the murderous objectivity of the Total State.

There is yet hope, which Jankowski holds fast to as the court of last resort of the hermeneutic enterprise—sometimes, it seems, against all personal and political odds. But hope rests on the idea of prayer as poetry, poetry as prayer, and both poetry and prayer at the heart—indeed, *as* the heart—of sturdy political action to not only resist but even to unseat any powers that wish to usurp one's heart and one's homeland. We saw this in its world-historical glory, and in truly Polish fashion, in the *Solidarity* movement, which was so key in bringing the Soviet Union down with a swiftness and a moral authority that excited a Polish Pope's blessing and that the threat of America's entire nuclear arsenal had never been able to accomplish. We see that same Walesa spirit in Jankowski's "Under God's Window."

POLAND AS POETRY AND PROPHECY

Under God's Windows

The highlander ancestors wail across time,
Hearing Slovak fiddles flying
Mated to driving rock and roll rhythms*
Demanding, we hear the lament of the dead.

Dig up that accordion out of Auschwitz's ashes,
Make the hurdy gurdy sing again.
This is not your grandfather's polka.
Visit Maria, transform your cynicism to voice of *suka*.+

Slavic brethren, you will not find *the answers* upon Tibet's plateau.
Put down the apple in your hand,
It is not the portal to our magic,
Or the Lady's miracles.

Walk out of your *Khrushchyovka* bunker^
Into the Carpathian Range.
We have been in the Iron Vale too long.#
It is time to ascend the *Gorale* trails.=

Feast on *oscypek* and glacial water.
Join your Polish kin
Under God's Windows
Where we of West and East are both set free by

The true sound of music.

* This was inspired by the Slovak Folk-Rock band *Hrdza*.
+ The Plock Fiddle (aka. The Suka) is the Polish ancestor to the violin.
^ *Khrushchyovka* is post-Stalin Era Soviet block housing.

John Keat's/James Hillman's vale of soul making.
= Gorale are particularly Polish Highlanders of the Carpathian Range.

HISTORY IS NOW—AND POLAND

For many poets, their country is not only a state but also a state of mind. It is not only a world-historical formation but also an ongoing array of psychic formations. It is not only a structure of power-arrangements in a political economy but Proust's "vast structure of memory" in the poet's psychic economy. Now as something fortuitous, now dire, depending upon the vagaries of history, how the poet "metabolizes" his country will, in almost all cases, be aesthetically influential. It will even be determining in some literary artists: Yukio Mishima in the 20th-century Japanese novel, Kipling in 19th-century British poetry, and Lessing in 18th-century German drama are good examples of that. Jankowski is very much in that tradition—and in a dual way as a Polish American.

This melding of memory, homeland, and psyche could hardly be otherwise, even—in a smaller but still similar figure—in the ordinary individual. This is the case because of the immensely articulated web of conditions that any social system must both endow and impose on its members in order to remain a going concern.

The declamations of anarchist political philosophy notwithstanding, most political philosophers from Aristotle to Rawls have taken it as a given that the human being is not fully human—is not, indeed, even possible—if he does not in large measure live, move, and have his being in an ordered state with a cultural history that, in its most robust forms, energizes and legitimates that nation-state. Without moorings in its history, a state is always in peril of a "legitimation crisis" (Habermas, 1975).

This is true of everyone. It is the poet, however, who makes higher spiritual sense of this fact and turns periods of cultural peril into possibility, just as the medieval Christian alchemist turned physical dross into metaphysical treasure (Jung, 1968). For the poet, his state is also a symbol, indeed one of his primary ones, and it is his culture that uniquely provides him with the historically- and geographically-molded archetypal images that define his work in time and space. They give those images heft and pull in locally rendering that morphic field called the "collective unconscious" (Bohm, 1997).

Examples abound. There is Ginsberg's howl against America, to which he protests he gave everything and received nothing in return, summoning the specter of an infinitely broader metaphysical vacuum that drives to "madness . . . the best minds of [his] generation"; Eliot's evocation of the sanctity of his mental England, where history comes to a climax, for "history is now and England" as he sits in "an empty chapel at smoke fall" and meditates on her transactions with transcendence.

This dynamic holds even in a specific region of a nation, as in Faulkner's fictional Yoknapatawpha County, where the deep poignancy but general mess of passion ornately plays itself out in despair and drunkenness, or, in contrast, in Williams's Patterson, New Jersey, chock full of people and things that are the seeds of his every idea, for "there is no idea but in things."

In all these cases, nation (fictional or actual, native to the poet or adopted by him) is not only political, it is poetical; not only what he knows best of time and space but also his conduit out of time and space in the archetypal images that a culture provides (Adams, 1996). Culture and the sacred are intertwined, like the two snakes moving up the caduceus.

For Jankowski, Poland is a pageant. Although an assiduous student of Polish history who commands an impressive knowledge of its factual record, for Jankowski, Poland is much more than just a chronicle; it is a cornucopia, so sensually abundant that—if fully appreciated, psychically taken in, duly honored—it becomes spiritually redemptive in its sheer plenitude and vibrancy. For Jankowski, there is no political reformation that is viable if it is not situated in Spirit, and Poland, still seeped in Catholicism, is today, as it has ever been, a bulwark (and sometimes the last one left standing) against an imminent demise of the West. (Again, the world-historical significance, indeed centrality, of *Solidarity*, and therefore of Poland, cannot be overstated.)

The death of the Western tradition Jankowski reckons a historical cataclysm—which is today not only announced but advanced at the contemporary university (product, though the university is, of a thoroughly Western history). The still evitable fall of the West would (if it comes to pass and all bets are that it will) be an unutterable tragedy.

It is a large part of Jankowski's purpose to call our attention to, then to decry, and finally to ardently resist this devolution into barbarianism ("The Barbarians are at the gate," it will be recalled, in "Our Lady's Cloak"). And while postmodernism sports in this wreckage and, not a little devilishly, urges it on in deconstructing whatever is precious, quintessential, and (if lost) unreproducible in the Western experience, Jankowski, in the tradition of the Polish knights and saints he reveres, writes poetic rites to salvage our now chronically ill culture, to help begin its *re*-construction into something finer than it ever was (Jankowski's hermeneutics of hope, again).

Hence, it is to history that Jankowski turns, and it is to its sacred lore and literature he calls out in order to craft a program of redemption for the future. In this, Jankowski is very like Jung, for, as I have written elsewhere,

> From the vantage point of the hermeneutics of hope, Jung called for revolution in response to the crisis of Western culture. . . . In a move that was conservative

and progressive, the Jungian revolution would entail inventing and experiment-
ing with one's entire life. . . . [However,] it would [also] require a return to the
narratives and symbols of a 2,500-year religious tradition of Western culture.
(Mayes, 2020).

"Under God's Windows" evidences from its outset this use of the past to gal-
vanize the present and redeem the future. In an introduction that is as much
an opening salvo as an opening stanza, Jankowski hears and attends to a fundamental fact, and it is that "the highlander ancestors wail across time." This
plangent call, this wail across the wall of history, is not an *idea* for Jankowski;
it is an *experience*; it speaks *to*, indeed it entreats the commitment *of*, the
whole person, not just polite but pallid intellectual assent from her.

Jankowski is not a fan of half-heartedness. As a poet, he gives to the reader,
and he requires from the reader, all in all. He does not care so much about
whether or not the reader agrees with him, although he is not indifferent to
that. What he does care about is that engaging him in his poetry will stimulate
the reader to care enough about her *own* cultural, historical, and spiritual life-
world that she will wake up and claim her life as her own—her own, that is,
in the sometimes raw and rugged, but ultimately redemptive interaction with
the Divine as she understands the Sacred (or better, as she *lives* it) through
the mediation of her culture. It is not a doctrine that Jankowski is trying to
implant in his reader; that is precisely the kind of thing he, like Jung (1966)
abhors. Rather, it is a passion—rooted in the "a sense of the holy" (Otto,
1958), morally manifested in the archetypal, and finally concretized in the
biographical and temporal—that he is trying to lure in wakefulness, and not
craftily but with "the lure of the transcendent" (Huebner, 1999).

For, he reckons it a poor thing to live any other way—as if life were a
Khrushchyovka bunker in which the person is just to eek out a life of dull
continuity, drab conformity to the awful edicts of the total state, stiffly delivered in the anti-language of political correctness, for some meager existential
salary in soiled epochal bills and greasy statist coins. The wail calls him,
claims him, and bids him call others, which he is now, by virtue of that call,
ethically obliged, dispositionally inclined, and aesthetically empowered to
do. Yet, how is the poet to accomplish this?

Not by diatribes. We get enough of those these days by social-justice-
warrior, tenured radicals on the Left who drive Lexuses and live in 3.2 million
dollar homes (with posters of Che on the walls) in gated communities; and
we get it as well from troglodytes for Trump or from the self-congratulatory
"Righteous," the self-appointed "Elect" of fundamentalism on the Right,
who preach love but pray for "Death to Fags." These things are anathema to
Jankowski, as all total political programs are. He will not *tell* us what it means
to be *a complex, uncategorizable, and committed individual in historical*

time and striving toward the shores of eternal time in the ship of his culture's world-historical time.

Rather, he will hold up for our scrutiny and instruction (the poet as pedagogue, again) the sad portraits of most people's dazed march through the uniform time of the state with its deadening agendas and dull ticks of the institutional clock. He will *show* us what it means to escape that. He will exemplify and embody it. He will not write poems about his life. His life will be about writing *poems.*

He will incarnate himself for the reader in his poetry's profuse imagery. He will dance his message for us in his poems variegated rhythm. He will do it whether that imagery and rhythm are *soothing*, as we "count lilies on the Virgin's cloak into untroubled dreamtime"; *shocking*, as when we are elbow deep digging through "Auschwitz's ashes" in search of a Hungarian violin; sad and slow, as if *laboring* through an "iron vale"; or ebullient as a hurdy gurdy, which the poet's very love of seems to resurrect, as it resurrects its peasant celebrants.

In each instance, the poet models for us, in his conundrums and commitments, what it means to live in the sacred as it manifests in one's culture—where, as in *A Midsummer Night's Dream*, transcendent vision is given "a local habitation and a name." Showing you this in his poetry, Jankowski wishes you to awaken to it in what can be the even greater poem of *your* life in *its* specific richness and idiosyncratic rhythms.

In Jankowski, the faithful, fateful celebration of Poland, *in* song, is of Poland *as* song, songs that are the heart of Poland's "vast structure of memory," as Proust characterized memory. And it is not memory of the past for its own sake in some sentimental exercise in fond futility that Jankowski is advocating for, but memory as a resource in knowing who one is: a creature of eternity whose negotiations with the world of mortality are perforce by means of the archetypal images that the culture bestows on its members. These the poet especially can summon up and deploy in battling the baleful ideological armies of the far-Right and far-Left—forces that would erase one's race, its particular signature on world-historical time, its rootedness in divine time.

These cultural legacies the poet can arm himself with morally in order to resist the de-culturizing, amoral momentum of transnational corporatism—neo-conservative or neo-liberal, it is all one)—which would negate all native narratives, to replace them with its non-narratives of individual and cultural uniformity in the service of a socially engineered wonderland of disenchanted comfort and vulgar plenty.

Memory is not primarily legal and probative. It is, rather, what we have of the past that arms us against the dull reign of triviality and terror that global strategists and transnational capitalists are planning for us in a socially engineered "One World" future. It is a dystopic scenario in which the only "difference" that will exist anymore is what kind of cog one is in the machinery of ungodly profit for occulted masters who are hell-bent on control of everything from how clouds drift around our globe to how synapses fire in the round of your skull.

Poland is thus also prophecy of how that incursion of impersonal collectivity on specific and "chrismed" cultural unities will be resisted (for it is the only way they *can* be resisted—by a specific people in unity of purpose) in the battles that lie ahead. Poland rises to her poetic vocation and political apotheosis (poetry and politics are inseparable in Poland) in the ecstatic exploration of her own iconic orbit, her own cultural and historical situatedness. This happens, to take the most signal example, in her devotion to the Catholic Church under the protective cloak and cosmic cleanliness of the Virgin, where you will be washed of the dross of the besotted postmodern and "transform your cynicism to voice of *suka*."

This restoration and resistance will come to pass in the celebration of Poland's blessed stubbornness that will allow no totalizing stranger to compromise her borders, or at least, not for very long, as bands of "Slavic brethren . . . ascend the *Gorale* trails" in a virile liberty; for, they will brook no bureaucrats to muzzle Poland's poetry in the insipidity of the "Official-ese" of some arrogant ministry or other or the defanged prose of a department of English. And it will happen in one's immersion in the sounds and smells and tastes that commemorate Poland's past as a bulwark of the West, yet in communion with the East.

Poland's musical and culinary celebrations of herself offer us all hope that it will continue to do the same in a future where there may be very little to celebrate and a great deal to lament. At least in lamenting, Jankowski suggest in the first stanza, we may become more teachable, more receptive to "the lament of the dead" for us—for what we have become, and even more distressingly, what we may yet become.

It is Poland's hope in herself, and our hope in in her, that she will not fail in her perennial connection with her history, her imperishable ability to always be manifesting the ancient and the venerable, in new ways, in a present that points her (and thereby points us, too) toward a meaningful future. And in memory of that and hope of that, the poet invites us all to "Feast on *oscypek* and glacial water" while hearing "the true sound of music" resound from the hills: the individual, embracing and being embraced by sacred cultural narratives, in tune and in touch with the divine thereby, and fortified to resist any total program, Right or Left, that would violate personal and culture autonomy and dignity in the light of the eternal.

And along with Jung, Jankowski does not believe that Eastern spirituality—despite the simple beauty and subtle efficacy of its psychospiritual technologies—or the *actual* technologies of the "apple in your hand" (a dual allusion to both the mythic root of sin in Eden and the potential for sin in the seductive products of Silicon Valley) will save us. We must save ourselves by finding ourselves again in reference to the sacral dimension of things that one's culture, in its purity, makes present, indeed makes possible.

It is not in the deconstruction of sacred narratives that liberty is found. It is, rather, in their reconstruction and further articulation in the creative crucible of history. It is not the erasure of history that sets us free. It is drawing *from* our history, honoring it (where it was honorable) and even dwelling in it, that vouchsafes us the vision to imagine an even richer, more realized future from the vantage point of a historically rooted, and therefore ethically stable present.

In "God's Windows," the conservative's reverence of the past and the progressive's zeal for the future, produce, in ancient dialectical fashion, a synthesis that preserves the virtues of each opposite and also transcends each opposite to arrive at a higher solution by attaining higher ethical and ontological ground. Jung (1969) called this "the transcendent function." Jankowski's poetry bears witness to the power of the transcendent function by manifesting it, incarnating it, in both the structure and themes of a sacred dualism that always resolves itself in a vision of the Divine, which we see, as it sees us, under God's windows on varied and verdant cultural landscapes.

Crucially, therefore, the poet is a teacher. He squeezes the last drop of meaning out of his culture, in the light and love of the Eternal, like Polish vinegar and sugar sauce over Kielbasa, to offer us up a tasty (and always tasteful!) sampling of his encounter with his culture. This he does not so that we may imitate it and him. For imitation, conformity, soul-soporific abstractions, and total political programs are what he strives against. He does it, rather, so that we, attending to his processes in confronting what Kierkegaard (1969) called "the curriculum of life," the true *currere,* will use his example as a model to remember, maybe even invoke, in engaging in similar processes in our own ways given our unique personal, cultural, and historical processes— all operating in the light of the Divine that shines through God's windows.

For, from those windows, a light issues that reveals the beauty of our diversity but also makes of it a unity in that it emanates from the Divine and returns to it, too. Here is a spiritual sociology, a transcendent multiculturalism that Jankowski proffers, whose source and goal, its alpha and omega, is, as in Hegel the Mind of God itself—not to be found in "Tibetan texts" (despite their loveliness and power as psychospiritual technologies) nor in the "apple in your hand" (a dual reference to both the sensual seductions of the Garden of Eden or the actual technological and virtual seductions of the

(ever ancient, ever new) that is sacred because it is, in turn enfolded, in the archetypal feminine cloaks of God.

"Visit Maria" is finally Jankowski's entreaty that we each rediscover the salvific feminine as it manifests in each culture uniquely. And Jankowski's appeal to his "Slavic Brethren" is finally, like Schiller's cry to all his "Brüder!," a reaching out to all men and women to join him in a historical dance to history's fulfillment in and as the Divine.

It is this call that variously but faithfully echoes in the poetry of Kyle Jankowski. Its fearlessness, rugged elegance, imagistic immediacy, and ethical electricity are bound to impress, and change, the reader.

REFERENCES

Adams, M. (1996). *The multicultural imagination: "Race," color, and the unconscious.* Routledge.

Buber, M. (1965). *I and thou.* Vintage.

Eliot, T. S. (2021). *The complete prose of T. S. Eliot: The critical edition.* Johns Hopkins University Press.

Habermas, J. (1975). *Legitimation crisis.* Beacon Press.

Hayek, F. (1944). *The road to serfdom.* University of Chicago Press.

Homans, P. (1995). *Jung in context: Modernity and the making of a psychology.* University of Chicago Press.

Huebner, D. (1999). *The lure of transcendent: Collected essays by Dwayne Huebner.* Lawrance Erlbaum Associates.

Jung, C. G. (1969). *Aion: Researches into the phenomenology of the self* (R. F. C. Hull, Trans.). Princeton University Press.

Jung, C. G. (1968). *Alchemical studies* (R. F. C. Hull, Trans.). Princeton University Press.

Jung, C. G. (1966). Fundamental questions of psychotherapy (R. F. C. Hull, Trans.). In H. Read et al. (Eds.), *The collected works of C. G. Jung: Vol. 16. Practice of psychotherapy* (2nd ed., pp. 111-125). Princeton University Press. (Original work published 1951) https://doi.org/10.1515/9781400851003.111.

Kierkegaard, S. (1969). *A Kierkegaard anthology.* R. Bretall (Ed). Princeton Press. University

Mayes, C. (2020). *Archetype, culture, and the individual in education: The three pedagogical narratives.* Routledge.

Otto, R. (1958). *The idea of the holy.* Oxford University Press.

Ricoeur, P. (1985). *Time and narrative.* Chicago: University of Chicago Press.

Stevens, W. (1990). *The palm at the end of the mind: Selected poems and a play* (H. Stevens, Ed). Vintage.

Tillich, P. (1987). *The essential Tillich: An anthology of the writings of Paul Tillich.* E. Church (Ed.). Macmillan.

Wertsch, J. (1985). *Vygotsky and the social formation of mind.* Harvard University
   Press.

About the Editors

Clifford Mayes is the author of 14 books and forty scholarly articles on educational psychology, multiculturalism, and curriculum theory. The founder of Archetypal Pedagogue, Mayes recently retired as a professor of educational psychology after over 20 years of service at Brigham Young University.

Jacquelyn Rinaldi received her doctorate in archetypal psychology from Pacifica Graduate Institute. Her teaching incorporates self-awareness as a key to humanity's next evolutionary step. She is currently completing her second doctorate in clinical psychology.

Ingram Content Group UK Ltd.
Milton Keynes UK
UKHW011257180423
420365UK00012B/41